W.B. Yeats
and
The Ideal of "Unity of Being"

W.B. Yeats
and
The Ideal of "Unity of Being"

Rajeshwari Patel

PRESTIGE

Published by
Prestige Books
3/28, East Patel Nagar, New Delhi 110 008
in association with
Indian Society for Commonwealth Studies
New Delhi

ISBN 81-85218-13-7

Jacket design by
3-A Corporation,
New Delhi 110 002

Phototypesetting by
data culture
New Delhi 110 065
Ph. 6431070

Printed at
Mehra Offset Press
New Delhi 110 002

To

Bhagawan Sri Sathya Sai Baba

Foreword

I would like to express my gratitude to Prof. C. Subbarao who is responsible, in many ways, for what I am, intellectually, today. I deeply value his perspicacious criticism of my work and his affection for me.

I am indebted to Prof. V.S. Seturaman who first introduced me to the poetry of W.B. Yeats. I had the rare privilege of being his student, and I am grateful for it.

To my dear parents, family and friends, I owe a debt of love. They have all been a constant source of encouragement to me.

There is a final debt, and it is an everlasting debt, which is due to the loving grace of Bhagawan Baba who has been an unfailing source of guidance and protection from the beginning.

Contents

Preface

Yeats is a poet who has come to occupy a central place in modern literature--so central that one cannot understand the age without a proper appreciation of his work. Familiar distinctions like that of "the man who suffers" and "the mind which creates" fail to offer an adequate explanation of the surprising vitality of his genius. As he got older, he showed an unflagging fertility and inventiveness and maturity which drew a fitting tribute from Eliot. Full-blooded and passionate, his unique and unmistakable voice, while restoring dignity and power to the Muse, "sweetened the brutal mouth of song" in the twentieth century.

With a deep understanding of the *zeitgeist* of the age, he spoke of its chief crisis as one of instability and a crumbling of the self, of a loss of connection. His own prophetic line from *The Second Coming*

Things fall apart; the centre cannot hold

offers a point of departure for the present study. Yeats was aware of the need for a unifying centre. Without it, there could be neither ceremony nor innocence. He abhorred "the filthy modern tide"– "the blood-dimmed tide," as he called it–and yet he stood out prominently from other poets whose voices strained to be heard despairing of the possibility of shoring the fragments of a broken culture. If in his apprehension of contemporary reality he often reveals a deep nostalgia for old, vanishing, far-off things, the texture of his nostalgia is far from *fin de siècle*, drawing vitality from the living voice of Irish tradition. Yeats's "version of the pastoral" cannot but be virile and affirmative in tone.

As a poet, his modernity lies not so much in daring experimentation, leading to a break with the past, as creative transformation of the essential and the continuing concerns of the romantic poets. Like the greater romantics, Yeats was fascinated by the enigma of the self, and the perils and the special challenges that it poses to the "last romantic" in the making of a poem. If out of a quarrel with ourselves we write poetry, the tragic struggle to overcome the divided psyche becomes the overriding concern of poetry. The poem could then become a paradigm for this predicament. But how is one to achieve unity, of any kind whatsoever, if the fierce contradictions refuse to be resolved?

Moreover, we would be forfeiting any claims to comprehending the problem if, knowing the complexities inherent in any attempt to integrate, we settle for a simpler solution than is permitted within the given premises. It is not so much a pull towards the "foul rag-and-bone shop of the heart," as a need to come to terms with its commonality, however difficult it may be, that makes "Byzantium" beside the Crazy Jane poems pose the deliberate question--Is it worth while to "scorn delights," look down upon life for the consolations of immortality? Caught between the dialectic of purity and pollution, the sacred and the profane, spirit and flesh, timeless and temporal, Yeats made a daring voyage to discover his "Swadharma" or unique identity. By plunging into the "abyss of self," making and remaking it, playing a variety of roles, by putting on and off a number of masks, he sought to make poetry and meaning in image and metaphor a temporary stay against confusion and anarchy. Declaring that--

> Words alone are certain good

--the wordsmith sought, and sought tragically, to fashion "an artifice of eternity" "in masterful images" purged of the taint of "the fury and the mire of human veins."

The poet is the exceptional man who makes meaning in the face of chaos. He freely moulds nature and human nature to suit his needs. Using the imagination in its capacity to create harmony out of discord, he achieves unity in terms of sameness and difference. In spite of Wordsworth's democratic claim that a poet is a "man speaking to men," Coleridge, and after him a host of others, made the freedom conceded to the poet's imagination a cherished value. This premium given to Imagination and its unity and order betrays an elitist orientation. While it may be true that the power to create, to forge a unity, is not without its hazards, the recreative act cannot be performed without the courage to see the true face of one's self. When art is made the exclusive and special field of extraordinary men, the politics of our notion of order can no longer be concealed.

With this kind of awareness, it is difficult not to feel self-conscious about dealing with a poet who made this same unity a quest of a lifetime, who believed in the aesthetics of the reformation and transformation of the self and life, and yet made existence the *sine qua non* of all meaning. What makes Yeats relevant to us is not any fake democratic stance, but that while he was an elitist when it came to style, form, etc., in everything else he was pledged to the human condition. He wanted unity but not by leaving "man" behind. Yeats's answer may not be the only one, but, in a sense, it is the true answer because it is an answer which rehabilitates Man.

The True Bearings of English Poetry

To understand the cultural crisis that has disturbed the essential harmony of life, we must look at our situation in the context of the whole human predicament. We have to shift our perspective from the second half of this century to a relatively static time-period from where the first faint signs of new, dynamic patterns of change began to appear.

From earliest times, man has been continually haunted by visions of unity, harmony, and the Golden Age. This deep longing seems to still survive in man, informing his proudest poetic aspiration and quest. Man could rarely resist the temptation to envision in myth, metaphor and song this persistent need to come to terms with the apparent disorder and chaos of ordinary human existence. While the first poets, assured of a shared set of beliefs and assumptions, could sing with "full-throated ease" and unself-conscious innocence, the modern poet, discomfited by the heavy burden of the past and the absence of a referential value-system, struggles to make meaning in self-conscious irony.

Though irony is the last thing that can ensure innocence, it is through irony that the modern poet would like to get beyond deception, attempt to recover "radical innocence," and restore the lost bearings of poetry. The fundamental problem is to discover a central, governing principle that can lend value to existence. The lack of an informing centre, whether we call it a frame of reference, a weltanschauung, world-picture, a received system of values, Degree of the Elizabethans,[1] or what the Indians refer to as "Dharma Chakra" or the wheel of dharma,[2] has a wide and varied impact on human life. Its ramifications may be seen in cultural history, the creative work of art, and the psychological drama of growing up—the self-conscious and traumatic struggle of the individual, "unfinished man" brought "face to face with his own clumsiness."[3]

Since in the absence of a unifying centre what results is dissolution, anarchy and disintegration, the unity may be, and is often, invented. It may be "made" as an act of creative exercise, without looking for any outward cultural norms or modes of conduct, by plumbing the depths within one's self. Yeats invoked "ceremony of innocence," wherein the "self-delighting, self-appeasing, self-affrighting" individual learns that "its own sweet will is Heaven's will" and can, though "every windy quarter howl/ Or every bellow burst, be happy still."[4]

Perplexed and troubled by the same problem, Wordsworth tried to put it affirmatively when, placing his faith in the regenerative and benevolent powers of Nature, he said:

> . . . for she can so inform
> The mind that is within us, so impress
> With quietness and beauty, and so feed
> With lofty thoughts, that neither evil tongues,
> Rash judgements, or the sneers of selfish men,
> Nor greetings where no kindness is, nor all
> The dreary intercourse of daily life,
> Shall e'er prevail against us, or disturb
> Our cheerful faith, that all which we behold
> Is full of blessings.[5]

An Arnold nostalgically recalled:

> The Sea of Faith
> Was once, too, at the full, and round earth's shore
> Lay like the folds of a bright girdle furl'd;
> But now I only hear
> Its melancholy, long, withdrawing roar,
> Retreating, to the breath
> Of the night-wind, down the vast edges drear

And naked shingles of the world.

Ah, love, let us be true
To one another! for the world, which seems
To lie before us like a land of dreams,
So various, so beautiful, so new,
Hath really neither joy, nor love, nor light,
Nor certitude, nor peace, nor help for pain;
And we are here as on a darkling plain
Swept with confused alarms of struggle and flight,
Where ignorant armies clash by night.[6]

The "ache of modernism" of which Arnold complained, the strange disease of modern life, with its "sick hurry" and "divided aims," split the old world wherein man had one business, one desire. Yeats, apprehensive of the consequences of this break, forebodingly declared:

Things fall apart; the centre cannot hold;
Mere anarchy is loosed upon the world,
The blood-dimmed tide is loosed, and everywhere
The ceremony of innocence is drowned.[7]

One may explain the fictions and frustrations, the pains and perils involved in this dilemma by historically dating it to the end of the Greek period or to the seventeenth century when, according to T.S. Eliot, a "dissociation of sensibility set in,"[8] or to some time before Shakespeare's birth when, Yeats believed, the fragmentation of western civilization occurred. It is not possible to indicate the exact period when the tragic break took place. But every poet and artist—one might even say every individual—longs for a golden age when the centre could hold and things did not fall apart as they do now. This longing is symptomatic of a basic nostalgia for unity, for original innocence, for roots.

The nostalgic dream of the recurrence of a happy past in a future time is reflected in every culture's cherished myth of an age in which man lived in harmony with himself and the community. Due to a marked attention of the western mind to matter and material existence, it may be more legitimate for a western writer to feel nostalgia for utopia. But the need to sustain the myth of unity is not peculiar to western culture. In the East, there is the concept of "Dharma." "Dharma" is regarded as something that holds together all human endeavour. The progressive decline of dharma is envisaged in the loss of balance by "dharmadevata," the god of dharma. The Indian concept of cyclical Time comprises four distinct ages—the Krita, Treta, Dwapara and Kali—each spread over some thousands of years. In the first age, the Krita Yuga as it is called, "Dharma" rested, it is said, on four "legs," and the centre was firm. One after the other, "Dharma" lost its "legs," and in the present Kali age it is said to be precariously balanced on a single "leg," suggesting the gradual loss of a sustaining idea of Unity.[9] The Indian example illustrates that the ideal of Unity, whether we look for it in a bygone era when there was apparently little or no isolation and division among men, or in some distant time in the future when man, hopefully, may attain Unity of Outlook, is common to all cultures.

Though it may seem unrealistic, one would still like to dream of an ideal period when poetry flourished and the creative writer did not have to face a hostile reading-public, suspicious of his bonafides. It is the aspiration of every artist to live and work in a congenial environment. Yeats wrote in *Essays and Introductions* that Blake said "all art is a labour to bring again the Golden Age, and all culture is certainly a labour to bring again the simplicity of the first ages, with knowledge of good and evil added to it."[10] For the artist, it means "a historical period possessing," as Kermode says, "the qualities they postulate for the image: unity, indissociability; qualities which, though passionately desired, are, they say, uniquely hard to come by in the modern world."[11] Yeats wrote in "Hodos Chameliontos" of how his interest in the arts and the sciences led him to "conceive a Unity of Culture defined and evoked by Unity of Image."[12] Yeats, like Cassirer and Wolf, seemed confident that human culture would progressively lead man to his self-liberation and that the paradoxical relation of illusion and reality, the savage and the refined, the ordered and the chaotic, the Apollonian and Dionysian would, through the experience of art, be momentarily resolved.

The impact of a breakdown or breach in a given culture, the loss of what Barfield calls "original participation,"[13] is felt in the arts, sciences and religion which stand proof of a new power acquired by man to build a world of his own. But it is at the personal level of man's uncertain, self-conscious journey from innocence to experience, involving his acquaintance with the "rites of passage," that its deeper impact may be identified. The psychoanalytical aspect of the problem of unity may be examined from the point of view of the metapsychology of Freud, Jungian individuation, and Yeats's theory of the mask, self and anti-self.

Sigmund Freud took the western world by storm when he explained, psychoanalytically, that man is born with savage instincts and dangerous, aggressive sexual propensities. He sought to account for the human predicament and the disintegrated self of man by means of what he called the "Oedipus Complex." He saw all reaching after meaning as a quest towards uroboric unity. Freud seemed to lean in the direction of culture as a symptom because he thought civilization is bought at the price of neuroses. Since man is relatively helpless, society must either tame him or perish. Kohut, on the other hand, feels that to explain human vulnerability in terms of the Oedipus Complex would be to treat a complex problem in a simplistic manner. He sees man as born ready to confront his surround in an active dialogue, creating his self as part of the world and the world as part of himself. Unlike Freud, he seems to favour the idea of culture as man's "expressed wholeness." Against the oedipal argument, his contention is that Hamlet's traumatic state arises from a temporary fragmentation of the self, the injured self fractured in its central values, or a "bipolar self with a shattered pole of ideals."[14] Applying this psychological idea to literature, Kohut comes close to defining the art which deals with the wounded self as modern art. As Joseph Frank puts it in *The Widening Gyre:*

> Art is no longer a miraculous gift of individual genius to mankind which creates a freedom from destiny. Now it is only a symbol that expresses man's collective and eternal struggle to transcend the conditions of his servitude.[15]

Is man in society the crippled victim of the socializing process? Are art, literature and religion symptomatic of the injury done to his naturally savage state, as Freud would suggest? Or, is he born incomplete, constantly striving to complete himself by interaction with his fellowmen and through an ever-expanding culture? Kohut feels that, even if man fails in the endeavour to achieve a culmination, there is no reason to despair. We ought to be "grateful for the fact that the disturbed wholeness of our self will never be fully or permanently restored" since "it is the very incompleteness of man's self, O'Neill's 'Man is born broken,' that spurs him to his greatest achievements, that keeps alive in him, to the end of time, the attempt to recapture the lost wholeness of his self."[16]

Jung went ahead of the Freudian contention that man is a natural savage. He professed the view that all creative products take their source from a transpersonal layer of the unconscious, an archetypal world—Yeats's "anima mundi"—which is a storehouse of knowledge closed to the conscious world. Creativity and culture express the collective problem of a whole people, and the way to integration involves a coming-to-terms with the collective psyche by striking a balance between conflicting impulses of the conscious and unconscious.

In subjective men, according to Yeats, art is the antithesis of what exterior fate snatches away. Their art is an attempt to overcome their internal struggles. What Yeats calls the "Mask" is "an emotional antithesis to all that comes out of their internal nature."[17] Art is born when "a nature, that never ceases to judge itself, exhausts personal emotion or desire so completely that something impersonal . . . starts into its place."[18]

The completed symbol cannot be realized without comprehending the struggles and the deep tensions in the single state of man. Dr. Jekyll and Mr. Hyde form the double name of man's single nature. They are the two faces of one individual in whom "the contraries are not mutually exclusive, but interdependent: 'harmony in contrariety, as in the case of the bow and the lyre'."[19] The conflicting elements cannot be reduced to a common denominator. If they are equal and opposite, they may balance each other out in a "co-existence of contraries," resulting in a dialectical unity. The productive tension is operative as separation as well as unification, and gives rise not to a static but a dynamic equilibrium. Since man is a union of matter and spirit, it would be futile to try to rise above the material element in our being. We would be going against the laws of our nature if we try to elevate one at the expense of the other, breaking the unity.

When Nietzsche, as Erich Heller writes, expressed a doubt if Europe would,

> after the end of the 'tragic' period of Greece, ever again know such reconciliation, and achieve so profound a harmony between the deepest and most conflicting impulses of the human soul

and wondered if we would ever be able to

> create an order which is not, as all our orders are, at the expense of the fullness of life, but its richest unfolding; a pattern which is not imposed over chaos, but overreaching and surpassing it, its beauty still tremulous with the ancient terror,[20]

he was not making a merely historical estimate, tracing the sharp break from a unified sensibility to the end of the tragic period of Greece. In his statement regarding the precarious quality of the unity achieved, Nietzsche endorses modern man's difficulty in creating an order that is not imposed but real, and which assimilates chaos even while transcending it—an order which is not achieved "at the expense of the fullness of life." Though brave and brilliant, Descartes's attempt to break the embodied spirit, but drawing a wedge between mind and matter, was doomed to fail right from the beginning since it disregarded the initial premise of the co-existence and interdependence of both in man.

The overwhelming question that confronts us in these considerations is whether we have posited a unity because man is genetically programmed to prefer order and balance. Is unity a real centre or a virtual axis around which we would like to build the edifice of our mental, spiritual and cultural life? And yet, whether real or imaginary, poetic or spiritual, the concept of Unity is indispensable to us. It serves as a yardstick by which we may measure both our failures and achievements.

Whereas religion was the cohesive force that upheld the centre once, Arnold sought to fill the void left by its absence by substituting art or poetry. We have come a long way, however, since Arnold declared his faith in the abiding qualities of poetry. According to him,

> The future of poetry is immense, because in poetry, where it is worthy of its high destinies, our race, as time goes on, will find an ever surer and surer stay. There is not a creed which is not shaken, not an accredited dogma which is not shown to be questionable, not a received tradition which does not threaten to dissolve. Our religion has materialized itself in the fact, in the supposed fact; it has attached its emotion to the fact, and now the fact is failing it. But for poetry the idea is everything; the rest is a world of illusion, of divine illusion. Poetry attaches its emotion to the idea; the idea is the fact. The strongest part of our religion to-day is its unconscious poetry.[21]

Arnold was not alone in professing such a faith. T.S. Eliot and, after him, I.A. Richards and a host of others pressed the point when they referred to the saving qualities of poetry. They were followed by others like R.P. Blackmur who said:

> Poetry is the *nous poetikos*, that deep habit of mind, deeper

than any sea of hope, calmer in its long swell than any mirror of despair, which imitates in forms and images dear to herself the life she has lived, the life she dreads to live, and the life she aspires to live.[22]

Philip Wheelwright simiiarly suggested that poetic truth, though contextual, is real, and can bring about the possible redemption of man through the fullest imaginative response. Deprived of the simple-minded religion of his childhood, Yeats turned to poetry, and created a mythic tradition of his own to sustain him through the growing sense of loss.

And yet, poetry has always been under attack. If the poet himself feels that his vocation is ineffective, that poetry is not "real," he becomes powerless before the recalcitrant forces of his times. Today, we are no longer certain of poetry's renovative powers. We feel that poetry may pass away, that it may not sustain Man. With the increasing commercialization of language, poetry may no longer occupy its high and important seat. Denys Thompson, concerned about this change, says:

> with the new prestige of science, 'scientific' precision became the model, so that the poetic potentiality of Elizabethan English came to an end. Poetry became literary.[23]

In other words, "poetry has lost confidence in itself and there is a widespread failure of human creativity."[24] Spiritual destitution has had a detrimental effect upon human culture and creativity. And, if this gradually deepening crisis seems to threaten our times in particular, it is because "the crime against life" belongs peculiarly to our own. Never has it been more widespread than in our technological civilization wherein the "emotionless emotions" of adolescents are mass-produced on television screens to do all the feeling for us. David Holbrook analyzes the problem in his *Lost Bearings in English Poetry:*

> The failure of confidence in poetry is not a consequence of a

failure of philosophy as an academic discipline. It is one aspect of a widespread failure of the personal philosophy of people at large, of day-to-day attitudes to existence in our civilization.[25]

In his early years, Yeats had a vague hope that Ireland "might be the first in Europe to seek unity as deliberately as it had been sought by theologian, poet, sculptor, architect, from the eleventh to the thirteenth century" if, instead of trying to "epitomize all human knowledge," "we first find philosophy and a little passion."[26] To live intensely and meaningfully appeared to be the solution. In the context of both philosophy and "intensity" failing, man himself has been put at stake, having lost faith in his ability to rebuild himself on a firm foundation. If poetry has suffered a temporary setback, it is a consequence of the wreck suffered by man to his centrality.

The baffling question is—When and how did the break take place? We admit the injury done to man's self, but we find it difficult to trace the wound to a specific historical time. It would even be preposterous to claim knowledge of the cause of the cartesian split. Nevertheless, a broad historical outline may provide a better perspective of the problem.

"Had not Europe," said Yeats, "shared one mind and heart, until both mind and heart began to break into fragments a little before Shakespeare's birth?"[27] The culture and life of Chaucer's time, like Yeats's imaginative world of Ireland, embraced "all, artist and poet, craftsman and day-labourer" so that they accepted a "common design."[28] Yeats wished his imagination would "somehow be rescued from abstraction and become as preoccupied with life as had been the imagination of Chaucer."[29] He believed that "if Chaucer's personages had disengaged themselves from Chaucer's crowd," "forgot their common goal and shrine, and after sundry magnifications" become "each in turn the centre of some Elizabethan play and had after split into their elements," they would have "given birth to romantic poetry."[30] It was, perhaps, "Somewhere about 1450, though later in some parts of Europe" and "in some earlier, men attained to personality in great numbers, 'Unity of Being,' and became like 'a perfectly proportioned human body,' and as men so fashioned held places of power, their nations had it too, prince and ploughman sharing that thought and feeling."[31]

The modern isolation between classes was not prevalent in Chaucer's world, in which man lived relatively at one with Nature, and life was viewed with wholeness. The world of the Middle Ages was "balanced in an internal play which does the work of holding in being a whole cosmic order,"[32] and "revealed, or invented, a coherence, a meaning, in the pattern of existence."[33]

Despite the impact of the Renaissance and the Reformation, this medieval view persisted and was, perhaps, carried over to the early seventeenth century when the first disturbing intimations began to emerge. Along with Puritanism, a general preoccupation of man with economic activity began to shake this solid view and threaten the unity of the world that Shakespeare celebrated. The transition from the Ptolemaic to the Copernican idea shook man's belief in the Earth as the centre of the Universe and the ground of his existence. The startling, hypothetical explanation that science gave to the origins of creation drastically altered what, hitherto, had been naively and unquestioningly accepted on religious authority.

> The new Philosophy calls all in doubt,
> The element of fire is quite put out[34]

says Donne, commenting on its impact on religion and society.

Perhaps the disintegration began in the Middle Ages when, as some say, a distinction—though not isolation—existed between the common and uncommon man. "Medieval European civilization," says Mason, "like most civilizations, had always known a sharp distinction between clerks and people, and there had been more than enough of tension between them. . . . The distinction becomes dissociation; the tension explodes into disintegration; and both these are new departures."[35] Eliot's argument that a dissociation of sensibility occurred in the seventeenth century appears preferential.

Though certainly useful for many reasons, it is not free from critical loopholes. By and large, however, we may safely say that from the early part of the seventeenth century onwards the world began to grow more confusing and disordered. The writer became correspondingly self-conscious about both writing and himself. As successors to the dramatists of the sixteenth century, the poets of the seventeenth century possessed a mechanism of sensibility that could devour of any kind of experience. In the seventeenth century, a dissociation set in from which, as Eliot says, we have never recovered.

If we were to go by the words of Whitehead who says that the concrete outlook of humanity becomes manifest in literature, and it is "to literature that we must look, particularly in its more concrete forms, namely in poetry and in drama, if we hope to discover the inward thoughts of a generation,"[36] we find in the literature of the early nineteenth century, especially its poetry, a clear indication of a discord between the aesthetic and the mechanical. As a reaction to this disturbing change, the nature-poetry of the romantic revival led a protest on behalf of the organic view of nature, a "protest against the exclusion of value from the essence of matter of fact."[37] With the agrarian revolution and rapid industrialization, life became more mechanized and impersonal. Man's significance in such a hostile world diminished, and he began to feel destabilized. Hitherto, he had been regarded as the epitome of all knowledge, power and beauty. Poets like Wordsworth attempted to revive the affinity with Nature that man had enjoyed earlier. Wordsworth, as John Press explains, saw the cosmic insecurity experienced by man reflected in the shifting pattern of the social order.[38] The lonely figures in his poetry are victims of a society which is no longer organically whole. Theirs is a fragmented world. For such as these, there can be no more the natural piety of a pagan; nor can the "heavy and the weary weight of all this unintelligible world" be lightened.

A "multitude of causes" contributed to "blunt the discriminating powers of the mind,"[39] making it almost impossible for the poet to discover meaning except through immense effort. Any meaning that he can wring out of the turmoil is, therefore, deeply poignant as it is earned at a great price, and after a struggle.

By reinstating the Imagination as a power which

> reveals itself in the balance or reconciliation of opposite or discordant qualities; of sameness with difference; of the general, with the concrete; the idea, with the image; the individual, with the representative.[40]

Coleridge made the aim of romantic poetry that of marrying the subject with the object, and arriving at unity from an apparent dichotomy through the image. To bridge the distinctions that disrupt social order, the poet has to forge the connections at a deeper level first. Thus, even while an initial dualism became a starting point—for romanticism everything depended upon "comprehending that unity which is at the same time duality, or conversely, the duality which is at the same time unity—within works, between works"[41]—what Coleridge and the other romantics wanted was a "monistic dualism" or a "dualistic monism."

The writers of the middle nineteenth century began with an acceptance of the dichotomy of subject and object, the natural and supernatural. But, whereas a poet like Wordsworth found

> In nature and the language of the sense
> The anchor of my purest thoughts, the nurse,
> The guide, the guardian of my heart, and soul
> Of all my moral being[42]

because he could perceive in the natural world

> A motion and a spirit, that impels
> All thinking things, all objects of all thought,
> And rolls through all things[43]

these writers could neither relate the natural to the supernatural nor the supernatural to the natural as the romantic poets had tried to do. If even Coleridge and Wordsworth, towards the end of their poetic career, expressed doubts about Nature's capacity to inhere meaning, it is a pointer to the painstaking effort involved in the struggle to sustain the balance.

The writers of the later nineteenth century could not conceive of a God who is both infinite as well as incarnate, as finite or immanent as well as transcendent. Even if God existed—which was, apparently, a remote possibility—He was no longer present in Nature. He appeared to have withdrawn
beyond the physical world. Yeats exclaimed that what was once a unity, one mind and heart, began to break into fragments.[44]

What had been for Arnold and Tennyson a withdrawal of God from Nature became, by the time we enter into the twentieth century, not only the disappearance of God—what Barfield refers to as "the withdrawal of Pan"—but death of the pathetic fallacy. A Nietzsche went as far as announcing: God is Dead.[45] The announcement reverberated all over the world. Nature was no longer a sympathetic participator in the human drama. It became merely a neutral, detached spectator. Since everything existed only in so far as the subject perceived it, even God became the object of man's knowledge, no longer its motivator.

Richards describes the disappearance of Pan in the twentieth century as loss of the Magical View. Yeats imputes this calamity to Science having driven out the legends, stories and superstitions that protected simple folk— "the immature, and the ignorant"—with symbol.[46] In *Poetries and Sciences*, Richards explains the "central dominant change"

> as the *Neutralization of Nature,* the transference from the Magical View of the world to the scientific, a change so great that it is perhaps only paralleled historically by the change, from whatever adumbration of a world-picture preceded the Magical View, to the Magical View itself. By the Magical View I mean, roughly, the belief in a world of spirits and powers which control events, and which can be evoked and, to some extent, controlled themselves by human practices. . . . Vestiges and survivals of it prompt and direct a great part

of our daily affairs, but it is no longer the world-picture which an informed mind most easily accepts. There is some evidence that poetry, together with the other arts, arose with this Magical View. It is a possibility to be seriously considered that poetry may pass away with it.[47]

In the catastrophe that has overtaken the old, organic world-view, poetry has become the first casualty. The neutralization of nature as a result of demythification has placed a considerable responsibility on the creative writer. Since the loss of the pathetic fallacy has deprived him of a vast treasure-house of material to draw from, a greater resourcefulness is demanded of him. His role is crucial and extremely challenging. His task is to save language from being commercialized, and, to preserve its semantic unity. It is only through an intelligent and careful use of language to express a complex experience, and the ability to dislocate, if necessary, word into meaning, that the writer may hope to revitalize its connotative power for poetic use. The poet is impelled to look "within" to find ways of making himself and his specific vision interesting and relevant. But when he does so, he sees nothing, or has no means by which to express satisfactorily what he sees. Looking into the heart of silence, he finds no words to speak his dearest wish or utter his deepest query. The propitious moment passes by without his being able to perform. The Orphic Mind in modern times is concerned, says Alvarez,

> in a worried way with the breakdown of traditions, and so prone to nostalgia for a lost classical culture—as in early Pound and Eliot. It would also be highly, self-consciously intellectual—as in Cubism or the Jesuit Cubist language of James Joyce or in the whole movement to reinstate the title 'Metaphysical Poet' as a fighting term.[48]

The predicament of the modern writer seems to parallel that of the metaphysical who felt the necessity to unify the intellectual and the emotional, the rational and the imaginative, thought and feeling.

Perhaps the modern period is the best time for poetry to flourish if, as Richards says, the poet accepts the situation and does not hold on to the Magical View that has become defunct. As a "sensitive and perceptive experience of the changing human situation" he should be "able to create within his work the pattern of a new order, which other men may learn from."[49] The poet must find a unifying image to achieve a momentary triumph over confusion, or else cease to be a poet. In the "death" of the poet, however, the world loses its Christ-figure, the scapegoat in whom all the sins of the world are continually re-enacted. The poet, by carrying the cross and the curse of "eternal return," becomes the means for the redemption of the world.

What inhered as unity of perception, in earlier times, changed with the arrival of science and technology. The scientific reductionist attitude brought the phenomena down to fundamental constituents and deprived man of a comprehensive world-view. This change was accelerated by the dissociation of word and meaning. The "Orphic character of language" which consisted in its "power of synthesis—in its ability to build up into form and idea that which is undifferentiated"[50] was lost. Science divested phenomena of the "last enchantments," as Matthew Arnold called it, or the magical view which had informed it. With it were removed the last traces of "original participation." The Darwinian classification of species in favour of a gradual evolution made the phenomena of nature "objects" that we unparticipated. For the

> generality of men, participation was dead; the only link with the phenomena was through the senses; and they could no longer conceive of any manner in which either growth itself or the metamorphoses of individual and special growth, could be determined from within. The appearances were idols. They had no 'within.'[51]

When words are used habitually even after their meanings have shifted, the poet, as an exceptional man, seeks to "purify the dialect of the tribe" by inventing new and fresh "images" to forge the lost connections and save language from bare, contextual meanings. The medieval mind—like the Vedic mind—saw everything symbolically, but the "physical" and literal meanings to which we are accustomed today have threatened to deprive the word of its multiple significance.

With his sense of rootedness and link with the past, the poet can become a path-finder. If he cannot restore "original participation," he can show us, at least, where "final participation" may lie. Thompson is confident that "poetry can put us in touch with the pre-logical mentality" that is thwarted in civilized men, and enable us to recover, what Charles Davy has called, the "participating consciousness."[52] Since the power of the poetic imagination "extends beyond the creation of song to the building up of a world"—the sphere of its activity being governed by an identity of word and being— "upon the ground of the poetic word," the "world can take on meaning and reality."[53]

The problem is not merely one of redeeming language. We need, first of all, a supportative philosophy or current of ideas to stem the tide of contemporary confusion. The dismemberment of Orpheus has crippled the lyrical bard. Life has become bankrupt of values. The philosopher must generate ideas and prepare the ground for the poet to work on. In his turn, the poet has to synthesize and shape, with the aid of the imagination, "unknown modes of being," giving them "local habitation and a name."

Unlike Dante, Spenser and Shakespeare, the twentieth-century writer lacks a philosophy or framework of ideas. This is evident in an absence of feeling, tenderness and sympathy. Due to a failure to relate, there is a failure to participate and, therefore, an inability to grasp one's identity. Even Arnold's "Ah, love, let us be true/To one another!" is called in question. In a world in which "encounter" or "meeting" is no longer possible, how can there be room for love? The schism in the modern personality has caused an emotional breach of reality. With very little to differentiate real life from fiction, even tragedy appears impossible. In the real life of daily play-acting, the curtain does not mercifully fall.

The new perspectives brought on by scientific advancement

have been achieved at the expense of the self. Due to an excessive over-reaching towards externalities, the devastating breach that has been made between the world and man has resulted in the collapse of his self. Paradoxically at the peak of knowledge about the physical and natural world, he is unable to return to the subjective realm, to undertake the shift of emphasis from the world to himself. Scientific reductionism, which has converted the world for specialist purposes into a conglomeration of colliding atoms or, at best, mathematical entities, has robbed man of his subjective centrality and given him an objective existence. The triumph of science has brought the world within man's grasp but his self has been threatened. Man has lost, in the process of trying to understand the laws of nature, his own bearings. Cleanth Brooks rightly states in his essay in honour of I.A. Richards:

> I venture to suggest that the modern writer's need to recognize and exploit tensional elements is ultimately to be connected with the present crisis in culture, that is, with the vast imbalance between means (science) and ends (values) and the consequent breakdown of traditional systems of value.[54]

Because he has permitted the rational and the logical apprehension of the world to supersede the imaginative, the "I" has become the nothingness of which the existentialisms complained. And while man is groping in the blind void of his own ego, it is not surprising that poetry has lost confidence in itself. Meaning has to be achieved by symbolizing, relating, and forging connections wherever possible. When this is not done, true feeling and genuine culture disappear. Resorting, in a spiritually barren society, to the stimulation of the instincts to give one a temporary feeling of pseudo-meaningfulness, we may promote a philosophy of despair. If Beckett, Sartre and others found man's life absurd and purposeless, it was because in their kind of existentialism the individual remained essentially alone, unable to interact.

Controlled, on the one hand, by external forces, man is subjected, on the other, to the governance of impersonal powers inside him. These, with their imperialistic sway over both the private and public self of man, curb his freedom to act creatively. Unable to transcend himself, the artist loses faith in the power of the poetic word. After all, "poetry makes nothing happen."[55] Placed beside the verifiable truths of Science, the non-verifiable "pseudo-statements" of poetry do not seem to stand much chance. As much ground as Science gains, it usurps from literature, making poetry feel always apologetical and need a defence to be made for it.

To accept with courage the anguish of making meaning in this kind of world means writing not a moralistic or didactic poetry but one that is deeply informed with life concerns, and engages itself with the complex philosophical and psychological situations that confront man. In a sense, our answer lies in the Romantics who, with the first impact of Science and rational thought on traditional beliefs, reacted by a deep preoccupation with the most fundamental problems of man. They asserted, in Blake's words, that "Without contraries is no progression," and aimed at a Coleridgean reconciliation of opposing and discordant forces into a productive unity.

Perhaps Arnold was the first modern who felt the pulse and ache of modernism. But like his scholar-gypsy, we can neither shun the world of man nor retreat to a world of make-believe. That kind of nostalgia would be debilitating. Eliot, in *The Elder Statesman,* said:

> I've been freed from the self that pretends to be someone
> And in becoming no-one, I begin to live.[56]

Though Eliot fell back on literary culture and anthropology, he could not cement the loss of belief, and give meaning to his world except by turning to a Christian past. And how many of us can do that? How many of us can say, like Ezra Pound, that we have "weathered the storm" and "beaten out my exile," when the exile is almost self-imposed? When man feels that "the imperfect social order is inadequate to resolve the inner conflict," he would look to something else, "search for a philosophy, a religion, a faith which will transcend and unify the felt disharmony."[57] But the comfort of a God or a philosophy that can ease the pain of isolation and alienation is denied to most of us. Yeats said:

> I was unlike others of my generation in one thing only. I am very religious, and deprived by Huxley and Tyndall, whom I detested, of the simple-minded religion of my childhood, I had made a new religion, almost an infallible church of poetic tradition, of a fardel of stories, and of personages, and of emotions, inseparable from their first expression, passed on from generation to generation by poets and painters with some help from philosophers and theologians.[58]

Yeats's unique answer, in the absence of faith in institutionalized religion, was the invention of a private mythology. If the poet is to find meaning, he must do so by standing on his own legs. As the "last romantic," Yeats responded by returning to the subject and restoring the primacy of the "I." However, Yeats's "I" is not the simple "I" of early lyrical romantic poetry. It is a complex "I" which chameleon-like changes colours and breaks into multiplicity, while retaining its essential "I-ness." And yet, even the Yeats who declared that there is "no truth saving in thine own heart"[59] found the borderline between truth and fiction very difficult to tackle. He thwarted Hic's aim to "find myself and not an image"[60] as being an unrealizable modern hope. By persistently attempting to strike an affirmative note, Yeats was trying to force, wring as it were, meaning out of meaningless confusion.

If poetry has to regain confidence in its powers, modern life being the complex thing it is, the poet/creator has to exercise an unrelenting Will and show extraordinary courage. As Arnold pointed out, "the creation of a modern poet, to be worth much, implies a great critical effort behind it, else it must be a comparatively poor, barren, and short-lived affair."[61] When traditional values and the past lose their validity and become superfluous, and there is no external canon to fall back on, the artist must plumb the depths within himself. Neither the poet who confines himself to an ideal world of his own, as did the French Symbolist, nor the aesthetician who ends up in pedagogic blindness, can restore wholeness. If the immense potentialities of art are to be realized, art must take into account the puny creature, "that forgotten thing, the normal active man"[62] of infinite possibilities.

With the only resource that remained, Yeats "set up a secondary or interior personality created out of the tradition of myself."[63] To discover the true bearings of the self and poetry, and "confess wrong without losing rightness"—he being his own enemy—the artist must reinstate the self, with all its strengths and weaknesses, at the centre. The logical corollary to personal authenticity is that one cannot then be false to "man." Putting the self at the centre means, of course, taking a great risk, personally at the least. But it is a risk worth-undertaking. Yeats knew that by playing God he would be threatening his own, perhaps brittle, integrity and courting poetic extinction. However, a failure of nerve would mean a failure to make any kind of meaning. If he is successful, the poet would not only have rehumanized the dehumanized self but also rehabilitated Man. For an answer which rehabilitates man, the price is bound to be high, as Yeats discovered. A man's courage is truly tested when he plunges into the abyss without hope of finding anything there, even the possibility of a return.

Yeats had been a vicarious participant in the cultural and political upheaval that shook the whole of Europe. Having gained a deep understanding of the zeitgeist and the troubles that affront the modern poet, especially the lyric poet, he could not but have embodied his self in art. Since he believed that the best part of him was in his work rather than in his life, his poetics made it imperative that he find his self through art or make his self a work of art—an "artifice of eternity."

In Yeats's poetry, therefore, we find the true bearings of English poetry restored. In it is given a hope of transcendence because it has not yet suffered the "death of sympathy." He would still find

> In all poor foolish things that live a day,
> Eternal beauty wandering on her way.[64]

In it, apathy is replaced by empathy, and there is participation both in the spiritual and the utterly human. In it is enacted the joy of art, and its tragedy, and creativity celebrated. The "fall into division" is acknowledged, and a "resurrection into unity" is visualized.

NOTES

1. William Shakespeare, "Troilus and Cressida," *The Complete Works of Shakespeare,* ed. W.J. Craig (1905; rpt. Oxford: Oxford Univ. Press, 1980), I, iii, 85-111.
2. Sankaracarya's *Self-Knowledge,* trans, Swami Nikhilananda (Madras: Sri Ramakrishna Math, 1978), p. 27.
3. Yeats, "A Dialogue of Self and Soul," *The Collected Poems of W.B. Yeats,* 2nd Edition (1950; rpt. London: Papermac, 1982), p. 266. Further referred to as *CP*.
4. Yeats, "A Prayer for my Daughter," *CP*, p. 214.
5. William Wordsworth, "Lines Composed a Few Miles Above Tintern Abbey," in *The New Golden Treasury of English Verse,* chosen by Edward Leeson (1980; 4th rpt. London: Pan Books, 1983), pp. 288-89.
6. "Dover Beach," *Ibid.*, p. 377
7. Yeats, *CP*, p. 211.
8. T.S. Eliot, "The Metaphysical Poets (1921)," *Selected Prose,* ed, John Hayward (1953; rpt. Middlesex: Penguin Books, 1955), p. 117
9. K.P. Bahadur, The *Wisdom of Vaisheshika* (New Delhi: Sterling, 1979), p. 3.
10. Yeats, *Essays and Introductions* (1961; rpt. London: Macmillan, 1971), p. 167
11. Frank Kermode, *Romantic Image* (1957; rpt. London: Routledge and Kegan Paul, 1966), p. 145.
12. Yeats, *Autobiographies* (1955; rpt. London: Papermac, 1980), p. 269.
13. Owen Barfield, "Original Participation," *Saving the Appearances: A Study in Idolatry* (New York: Harcourt Brace Jovanovich), pp. 40-41.
14. Cited from Ernest S. Wolf, "Psychoanalytic Psychology of the Self

and Literature," *New Literary History,* Vol. XII, No. 1 (Autumn 1980), p. 51.

15. *The Widening Gyre: Crisis and Mastery in Modern Literature* (Bloomington and London: Indiana Univ. Press, 1963), p. 118.
16. Ernest Wolf, p. 53.
17. Yeats, *Autobiographies,* p. 189.
18. *Ibid.*, p. 332.
19. Ernest Cassirer, *An Essay on Man: An Introduction to a Philosophy of Human Culture* (New Haven and London: Yale Univ. Press, 1944), p. 228.
20. "Rilke and Nietzsche," *The Disinherited Mind: Essays in Modern German Literature and Thought* (London: Bowes and Bowes, 1971), p. 136
21. "The Study of Poetry," in *The Oxford Anthology of English Literature,* Vol. II, ed. Frank Kermode and John Hollander (London: OUP, 1973), pp. 1019-20.
22. *The Lion and the Honeycomb* (New York: Harcourt, Brace, 1954), p. 297
23. *The Uses of Poetry* (Cambridge Univ. Press, 1978), p. 208.
24. *Lost Bearings in English Poetry* (London: Vision Press, 1977), p. 11
25. *Ibid.*
26. Yeats, *Autobiographies,* p. 195.
27. *Ibid.*, p. 191.
28. *Ibid.*, p. 194.
29. *Ibid.*, p. 188.
30. *Ibid.*, p. 193.
31. *Ibid.*, p. 291.
32. Michael Mason, "Game and Earnest," *The Centre of Hilarity: A Play Upon Ideas About Laughter and the Absurd* (London: Sheed and Ward, 1959), p. 79.
33. John Press, *The Chequer'd Shade: Reflections on Obscurity in Poetry* (London: OUP, 1963), p. 109.
34. "An Anatomie of the World: The First Anniversary," in *The Poems of John Donne,* ed. Sir H.J.C. Grierson (London: OUP, 1945), p. 213.
35. Michael Mason, p. 120.
36. Alfred North Whitehead, *Science and the Modern World: Lowell Lectures, 1925* (New York: Mentor Book, 1956), p. 76.
37. *Ibid.*, p. 96.
38. John Press, p. 112.

39. "Preface" (*Lyrical Ballads,* 1802), *Selections from Wordsworth: Poetry and Prose,* ed. Sir Ifor Evans, 11th Edition (1935; rpt. London: Methuen, 1966), p. 185.
40. *Biographia Literaria,* ed. George Watson (1975; rpt. London: J.M. Dent, 1977), p. 174.
41. Raymond Benoit, *Single Nature's Double Name: The Collectedness of the Conflicting in British and American Romanticism* (Paris: Mouton, 1973), p. 12.
42. Wordsworth, "Lines," in Edward Leeson, p. 288
43. *Ibid.*
44. Yeats, *Autobiographies,* p. 191.
45. Octavio Paz, in his *Children of the Mire: Modern Poetry from Romanticism to the Avant-Garde, trans.* Rachel Phillips (Cambridge: Harvard Univ. Press, 1975), p. 25, makes an interesting case. In his words: The dispute between reason and revelation also tore the Arab world apart, but there the victory went to revelation: the death of philosophy and not, as in the West, the death of God. Eternity's triumph shut the gates of the future, and identity won an absolute victory: Allah is Allah. The Western world escaped tautology only to fall into contradiction.
46. Yeats, *Selected Criticism and Prose,* ed. A. Norman Jeffares (London: Pan Books, 1980), p. 212.
47. *Poetries and Sciences,* a Reissue of Science and Poetry (1926, 1935) with commentary (London: Routledge and Kegan Paul, 1970), p. 50-51.
48. A. Alvarez, *Beyond All This Fiddle: Essays 1955-1967* (London: The Penguin Press, 1968), p. 3.
49. Cited from Stephen Spender, *The Making of a Poem* (1955; London: Hamish Hamilton, 1957), p. 21.
50. Gerald L. Bruns, *Modern Poetry and the Idea of Language: A Critical and Historical Study* (New Haven: Yale Univ. Press, 1974), p. 211.
51. Owen Barfield, p. 63.
52. Denys Thompson, *The Uses of Poetry,* p. 202.
53. Gerald Bruns, p. 207.
54. "I.A. Richards and the Concept of Tension," in *I.A. Richards: Essays in His Honour,* ed. Reuben Brower, Helen Vendler, and John Hollander (New York: OUP, 1973), p. 135.
55. W.H. Auden, "In Memory of W.B. Yeats," in Edward Leeson, p. 462.

56. "The Elder Statesman," *Collected Plays* (London: Faber and Faber, 1962), p. 354.
57. Jacques Barzun, *Classic, Romantic and Modern* (Chicago: The Univ. of Chicago Press, 1961), p. 17.
58. Yeats, *Autobiographies*, pp. 115-16.
59. Yeats, *CP*, p. 8.
60. *Ibid.*, p. 180.
61. "The Function of Criticism at the Present Time," *Matthew Arnold's Essays in Criticism* (1st and 2nd Series), introduced by G.K. Chesterton (1906; rpt. London: J.M. Dent, 1969), p. 12.
62. Yeats, *Autobiographies*, p. 492.
63. *Ibid.*, p. 463.
64. Yeats, *CP*, p. 35.

Of Man and the Masks

In his address to the British Association in September, 1908, Yeats made a few remarks that nearly sum up his philosophy of life. Mankind, he said,

> must be seen and understood in every possible circumstance, in every conceivable situation. There is no laughter too bitter, no irony too harsh for utterance, no passion too terrible to be set before the minds of men. The Greeks knew that. Only in this way can mankind be understood, only when we have put ourselves in all the possible positions of life, from the most miserable to those that are so lofty that we can only speak of them in symbols and mysteries, will entire wisdom be possible.[1]

Thomas Parkinson writes about Yeats that his basic insight

> into the modern mind is that it is best understood as a battleground of contending and only temporarily reconcilable forces. His theory of history—really his "psychology" of historical types—embodies that view.[2]

When a poet has neither a fundamental intellectual certainty or belief to hold on to, nor even the certainty of doubt to fall back on, the poetic impulse would

> be in danger of breaking under a burden too heavy for its delicate constitution. This danger will arise when the poet, compelled by the peculiar spiritual barrenness of his age, has

> to struggle for the poetic expression of unheard-of and unthought-of experiences.[3]

Yeats had, as Eliot said, a courage that was rare for a man of his times, a courage that came from a determination to do what he thought was worth-doing. In a worthy venture, no effort was too expensive. He considered his art more important than anything else, and was, therefore, willing to take any risk on its account. He cared more for poetry than for his reputation as a poet, or the picture of himself as a poet.[4] Art was greater than the artist, greater than himself.

Defending his revision of earlier poems, he said:

> My friends that have it I do wrong
> Whenever I remake a song
> Should know what issue is at stake
> It is myself that I remake.

He was no idle poetaster. He had put his life into his poems, and to make them he had broken his life "in a mortar as it were." Standing detached from his own life, he would look at it from a distance—"Commenting, commenting."[5] His close friend, Katharine Tynan, found that "he had an uncanny faculty of standing aside and looking on art, the game of life, as a spectator."[6] A self-critic, Yeats was not satisfied with the safe and the agreeable. He was prepared to hazard self-exposure rather than avoid a difficult solution to a complex conflict. He was man enough to look inside himself for answers to fundamental questions. "Why should we honor," he said, "those that die upon the field of battle, a man may show as reckless a courage in entering into the abyss of himself."[7]

For Yeats, the Poet came before the Hero, not the Hero before the Poet. In fact, he could see no distinction: the poet is hero. Yeats did his writing by "self-distrusting reasons" because he felt one should not make a false faith by concealing from one's own thoughts the causes of doubt. As "faith is the highest achievement of the human intellect, the only gift man can make to God," it must be offered in sincerity:

> Neither must we create, by hiding ugliness, a false beauty as our offering to the world. He only can create the greatest imaginable beauty who has endured all imaginable pangs, for only when we have seen and foreseen what we dread shall we be rewarded by that dazzling, unforeseen, wing-footed wanderer.[8]

Talking of Lionel Johnson, Yeats said that a poet is a man who, by the nature of things, lives with entire sincerity. The "better his poetry the more sincere his life."[9] His life is an experiment in living, and all those who come after him have a right to know about it. It is the duty of a lyric poet, whose "poetry is no rootless flower but the speech of a man,"[10] to give his "life" as well as his "words" to the criticism of the world.

Yeats's practice of putting an actual situation into art rested on the belief that the struggle for complete affirmation may be, often is, that art's chief poignancy. And by "actual situation" he did not mean life in its crude, raw state. Yeats's idea of sincerity has to be understood with certain qualifications. In the arts, it is style. In life, it is courtesy and self-possession. Both "arise out of a deliberate shaping of all things, and from never being swept away, whatever the emotion, into confusion or dullness."[11] Sincerity does not mean writing out one's emotions exactly as they occur, without altering or shaping them to make them more beautiful. Yeats's own poetic practice suggests that art was not a mere imitation of life. Making "passion" the formative power of art, one must give form and shape to what is chaotic and unformed.

Unlike the rhetorician who deceives his neighbour, and the sentimentalist himself, the artist's passion is for reality. To arrive at this reality through the via media of a quarrel with one's self, the lyric poet must work towards making "All sounds, all colours, all forms" which "either because of their preordained energies or because of long association, evoke indefinable and yet precise emotions," through a "musical relation, a beautiful relation to one another," become "one sound, one colour, one form, and evoke an emotion that is made out of their distinct evocations, and yet is one emotion."[12]

In prefatory remarks to a volume of his collected poems, Yeats added an apologia which is a testimony of his renewed efforts to remake himself and his art. All art, he said,

> is in the last analysis an endeavour to condense as out of the flying vapour of the world an image of human perfection, and for its own and not for the art's sake, and that is why the labour of the alchemists, who were called artists in their day, is a befitting comparison for all deliberate change of style.[13]

Yeats's insistent claim that poetry is a means toward self-knowledge may sound trite to those of us who go through life and its dailiness of living without ever confronting the real self. We can hardly understand a man's life-long preoccupation with the discovery of the self beneath each mask.

When Yeats wrote—

> Turning and turning in the widening gyre
> The falcon cannot hear the falconer;
> Things fall apart; the centre cannot hold;
> Mere anarchy is loosed upon the world[14]

—he was not merely referring to a change of historical cycles. The poem, *The Second Coming,* cannot be treated as a simple statement on history. Yeats was perhaps also suggesting that the loss of one's bearings may result in inner anarchy and turmoil. This can eventually lead to a notional confusion in man's thinking, and understanding of the self. In a manuscript, Yeats affirmed:

> My character is so little myself that all my life it has thwarted me. It has affected my poems, my true self, no more than the character of a dancer affects the movements of a dance.[15]

Yeats appears to be making, here, a distinction between the real self and, what he calls, his "character." For a poet who has chosen to conceal the true self beneath the mask, this distinction may allow a false projection to appear more real than the real self. But Yeats seemed willing to take the chance. He had the extraordinary courage and ability to look into the "mirror" and accept truthfully what he saw there.

Yeats said that he had put his self in his poetry. But, once it entered the work of art, it did not remain the crude, unformed, naked self that speaks across the breakfast table. If one wrote of

> personal love or sorrow in free verse, or in any rhythm that left it unchanged, amid all its accidence, I would be full of self-contempt because of my egotism and indiscretion, and foresee the boredom of my reader.[16]

In a general introduction to his work, Yeats gave us the first principle:

> A poet writes always of his personal life, in his finest work out of its tragedy, whatever it be, remorse, lost love, or mere loneliness; he never speaks directly as to someone at the breakfast table, there is always a phantasmagoria. Dante and Milton had mythologies, Shakespeare the characters of English history or of traditional romance; even when the poet seems most himself . . . he is never the bundle of accident and incoherence that sits down to breakfast; he has been reborn as an idea, something intended, complete. . . . He is Lear, Romeo, Oedipus, Tiresias; he has stepped out of a play, and even the woman he loves is Rosalind, Cleopatra, never The Dark Lady. He is part of his own phantasmagoria.[17]

Moreover, it is only through self-expression of the whole man that an impersonal mythology can emerge:

> Does not all art come when a nature, that never ceases to judge

itself, exhausts personal emotions in action or desire so completely that something impersonal, something that has nothing to do with action or desire, suddenly starts into its place, something that is as unforeseen, as completely organized, even as unique, as the images that pass before the mind between sleeping and waking.[18]

When a poet puts his faith into words and tries, more and more, for self-portraiture, he must take care to make the self he portrays convincing and credible. Given the complex nature of contemporary experience, he cannot write about himself without being accused of insincerity, affectation, and a certain lack of moderation. He is liable to be mocked at by the world, and denigrated as a poseur. When a modern poet, especially, begins to speak about himself, he automatically feels self-conscious. He is uneasy, and afraid he may appear pretentious and fake. It is difficult for him to acquire a speech "so natural and dramatic that the hearer would feel the presence of a man thinking and feeling."

Against the philistinism of the "practical" man, the artist has little hope of being left unscathed. No-one was more aware of this predicament of the poet than Yeats. He took his art very seriously, and knew that, in a world governed by standards different from his own, the lot of the artist is isolation and alienation:

> A line will take us hours maybe;
> Yet if it does not seem a moment's thought,
> Our stitching and unstitching has been naught.
> Better go down upon your marrow-bones
> And scrub a kitchen pavement, or break stones
> Like an old pauper, in all kinds of weather;
> For to articulate sweet sounds together
> Is to work harder than all these, and yet
> Be thought an idler by the noisy set
> Of bankers, schoolmasters, and clergymen
> The martyrs call the world.[19]

The more Yeats tried to make his art deliberately beautiful, the more he found himself following his opposite,

> For deliberate beauty is like a woman
> always desiring man's desire.[20]

Accordingly, he developed a theory of poetry that would lead to a fuller realization of himself, relying on conflict as a formative principle of poetic expression. Yeats saw the inevitable discrepancy between art and life, and between his present and future self. His need to take up a number of "traditional poses," even his attempts at poetry-making, were grounded in a deep compulsion within himself to blend the ideal with the real world. While in his early verse he sought an escape from the actual day-to-day world by flying to isles of bliss and gaiety, in the later, maturer poetry he began, like Nietzsche, to reject the real world, with its vulgar, democratic ideals, and prefer the natural aristocracy of men whose ideals are nobler and "not of this world." In other words, what was a basic conflict right from the beginning, became a strong motivating principle of his later work when the conflict converted itself into an artistic strategy based on the idea of self and anti-self. The problem was to resolve the conflict present in the consciousness by means of a dialectical tension, leading to unity. One cannot talk meaningfully about conflict without simultaneously conceiving its possible resolution. A poem about integration, for example, must enact conflict within the poetic structure before it can offer a convincing evidence of the reconciliation achieved.

Yeats reversed the nineteenth-century idea that a man finds his identity through self-realization. He established the contrary truth that being true to one's self means becoming one's opposite, all that one abhors. Yeats recognized that the central concept of the psychology of Jung was the process of individuation, a reconciliation between the opposite forces of the conscious and the unconscious into a new balance within man's own psyche. Jung named the new centre, which is neither conscious nor unconscious, the "self." The anti-self, the opposite of the conscious self, was called the "shadow." It personified all that we do not like to admit about ourselves. Since we do not want to own up this dark side of our nature, we prefer to think of it as being outside ourselves. Though it is a "dark brother" and, in truth, a part of us, we wish to keep it hidden. In an attempt to come to terms with it, we often externalize it in imaginary figures like Satan, Caliban, Hyde, and so on.[21] Individuation, in Jungian terminology, involves our becoming aware of this "shadow," and accepting its inevitable presence in us without shock. For Yeats, this meant a state in which man is capable of remaining in uncertainties, mysteries, and doubts, without any irritable reaching after fact and reason. Assimilating the concept of self and anti-self to his theory of the mask, Yeats sought to achieve, through art, not only poetic integration, but also integration of the personality. In stating that "Eternity expresses itself through contradictions" and "Talent perceives differences, genius unity," Yeats was not voicing banal platitudes. To him, the problem of Unity acquired a moral, spiritual and artistic dimension.

The division into two contradictories, as Read explains,

> corresponds with a polarity that runs throughout nature and history.... The dialectic of the life process is based upon this fact, and yet in our conscious practical life, we try to hide the fact. We think of ourselves as single in consciousness, of one sex, and generally as wholly good in intentions. But this illusion of unity does not correspond with the reality.[22]

Valery believed that "if each man were not able to live a number of other lives besides his own, he would not be able to live his own life." Yeats also mentioned in his diary of 1909:

> There is a relation between discipline and the theatrical sense. If we cannot imagine ourselves as different from what we are and assume that second self, we cannot impose a discipline upon ourselves, though we may accept one from others.[23]

This kind of discipline is essential, as Yeats learnt, for a man who wishes to write lyric poetry, because then he must be shaped by nature and art "to some one out of half a dozen traditional poses, and be lover or saint, sage or sensualist, or mere mocker of all life."[24]

In an essay entitled "Poetry and Tradition," Yeats writes that the "nobleness of the arts is in the mingling of contraries, the extremity of sorrow, the extremity of joy."[25] Conflict may be present not only within the mind of the poet, but also in something that exists outside and yet makes up the poem. Yeats told Ethel Mannin that to him all things are made of the conflict of "two states of consciousness, beings or persons which die each other's life, live each other's death,"[26] and that he had found his peace by putting his "sole nature against something and the greater the tension the greater my self-knowledge."[27]

Yeats had read Blake and Nietzsche, and their ideas left a deep impression upon his mind. Blake in *The Marriage of Heaven and Hell* said,

> Without contraries is no progression—
> Attraction and repulsion, reason and energy,
> love and hate, are necessary to human existence.[28]

Blake's "Without contraries is no progression" may be juxtaposed with Yeats's "consciousness as conflict" and the concept of self and anti-self. Nietzsche and Yeats share a common belief in the religion of art, a belief so staunch that it tends to blur the distinction between the aesthetic and the moral. Lorna Reynolds enumerates the extensive debt that Yeats owes to Nietzsche:

> Such ideas as the essential unity of the human being, the falsity of the long-held dichotomy between body and soul, the passing of extremes one into another, the transcendence of established values, the need for the mask for self-understanding, the necessity to surpass oneself, satisfaction not as residing in the thing achieved but in the achieving, the concept of heroic joy, salvation from life's suffering through

> creation, the need for much suffering and much transformation before the creator can appear, the dance as the greatest expression "of life's meaning," the admiration for the aristocratic virtues and contempt for the "populace," the crookedness of the pathos of wisdom, the inescapable duty of self-expression.[29]

—all these Nietzschean overtones are found assimilated into the Yeatsian.

Though, like Nietzsche, Yeats put his faith in the power of the word, when the formative unity of a work of art is given a moral complexion, it can pose several problems. One may accept the initial premise of a conflict or discord, but that does not minimize the task of the imaginative faculty. The imagination has to bring the antithesis back into a unity. In other words, the artist has to preserve the "integrity of his soul" even while he apparently indulges in contradictions by taking upon himself half a dozen "traditional" poses. Yeats's theory of the mask, as enunciated in *Anima Hominis,* becomes a natural corollary to this basic idea of moral and poetic integration. Yeats knew that in his rejection of the real world he would lose grasp of the more complex world, and

> Someday setting out to find knowledge, like some pilgrim to the Holy Land he will become the most romantic of characters. He will play with all masks.[30]

According to Yeats, all happiness depends on the energy to assume the mask of some other life,

> on a rebirth as something not one's self, something created in a moment and perpetually renewed; in playing a game like that of a child where one loses the infinite pain of self-realization, in a grotesque or solemn painted face put on that one may hide from the terror of judgement.... Perhaps all the sins and energies of the world are but the world's flight from an infinite blinding beam.[31]

What distinguishes "active virtue" from the "passive acceptance of a current code" is that it is "consciously dramatic, the wearing of a mask."[32] Therefore, Yeats aimed at a resolution of the problem of poetic integration by adopting a number of roles, even if it meant risking personal integrity in the confusion of multiple voices. His "poetry of dialogue" is a direct result of this idea. In the early period, conflict was externalized. In poem after poem, the poet took on the mask of a figure or character drawn from Irish legendary history. A maturer perception brought the conflict to inhere in a single poem, enacting itself as a dialogue of confrontation between two selves or two voices.

When the artist seeks an image, not a book, not the imitation of great masters who, after all, "own nothing but their blind, stupefied hearts," he would, on awakening from the "common dream,"

> . . . call to the mysterious one who yet
> Shall walk the wet sands by the edge of the stream
> And look most like me, being indeed my double,
> And prove of all imaginable things
> The most unlike, being my anti-self.[33]

It is only he who despairs of the world, and out of his tragic vision has come closer to reality, that sings. The rest who are driven and lured by the "common dream," and love the world, do not write or paint. They "grow rich, popular and full of influence." They do not sing. They cannot—only the artist who has seen the "vast desolation" can do that. The lot of the common man is to serve the world in action. His life is but

> The struggle of the fly in marmalade.[34]

It is when one calls to one's opposite, summoning all that one has handled least, least looked upon, that one can find one's self. It is by moving away from the self that one, paradoxically, discovers one's self. As embodied in the biblical paradox:

> He that findeth his life shall lose it: and
> he that loseth his life for my sake shall find it.[35]

Certain men as Synge, Dante and Keats recognized in their art not only an opposing virtue but also a "compensation for some accident of health or circumstance."[36] A man condemned to the life of a monk by bad health, such as Synge was, would take an amused pleasure in "great queens." In Synge's art one finds his imagination delighting in fine physical health because that was the one thing most denied to him:

> The last act of *Deirdre of the Sorrows,* where his art is at its noblest, was written upon his death-bed. He was not sure of any world to come, he was leaving his betrothed and his unwritten play.[37]

Naturally, he hated to die, and yet

> in the last speeches of Deirdre and in the middle act he accepted death and dismissed life with a gracious gesture. He gave to Deirdre the emotion that seemed to him most desirable, most difficult, most fitting, and maybe saw in those delighted seven years, now dwindling from her, the fulfillment of his own life.[38]

Dante celebrated the "most exalted lady loved by a man"

> not merely because death took that lady and Florence banished her singer, but because he had to struggle in his own heart with his unjust anger and his lust; while, unlike those of the great poets who are at peace with the world and at war with themselves, he fought a double war.[39]

To the question as to whether there are not poets who have made their art out of sheer joy—poets like Keats, whom we remember for his "deliberate happiness"—Yeats's answer is, in Hic's words,

> His art is happy, but who knows his mind?
> I see a schoolboy when I think of him,
> With face and nose pressed to a sweet-shop window,
> For certainly he sank into his grave
> His senses and his heart unsatisfied,
> And made—being poor, ailing and ignorant,
> Shut out from all the luxury of the world,
> The coarse-bred son of a livery-stable keeper—
> Luxuriant song.[40]

Yeats's *A Vision* is also based, as Melchiori summarily puts it, on the idea that conflict governs all existence. Every human being is expressible as both himself and his mask. What is characteristic of individuals is exemplified by historical periods which belong likewise "to opposed principles: the principle of objectivity, which Yeats calls *primary* and that of subjectivity, which he calls *antithetical.* In between these two extreme conflicting poles there are a number of possible intermediate states."[41]

Cuchulain wears a "lonely, imperturbable proud mask" as a kind of protection because he is "overwhelmed with the thought of his own weakness." The proud and the weak, as opposites, are there in every man because "all things fall into a series of antinomies in human experience."[42] But these may be temporarily resolved by externalization and objectification. Like Synge, Yeats cured his own particular ailment—the sense of humiliation that he carried through his early life—by writing of proud and confident men and women.

There was, however, a deeper urge of the artist and the man that needed to be satisfied—the passionate, almost poignant, impulse to know the reality of the self and the world. A man is simply a man. But Yeats's poet is "more type than man, more passion than type,"[43] and can, with the power of creative transformation, make himself anew. Applying this imaginative idiom, even his Ireland, his Poet, and his Self are a fiction. If he wrote of proud and confident men, it was not because he had any ambition for political power. Yeats wanted power. But it was moral power, self-mastery, self-definition, the ability to transform experience that he wanted in order not to remain helpless before the "contents of his own mind." Since rhetoric was the governing art in Ireland, and "proof of power is voice," value is ascribed to gesture. Style is the passion with which the poet performs his role.

Would not a poet who finds with the coming of old age that he cannot keep his mask without "new bitterness" and "new disappointment" be compelled, having lost his vigour, to lose the favour of his muses?[44] Would he not cease to exist as a poet? Yeats did not think that the struggle to achieve integration, or what he called Unity of Being, could be contained in a single human existence, and end with death. He, therefore, upheld a theory of history based on the philosophy that human perfection can be achieved only over a number of lives. Every man must pass through different "phases of the moon" before he can reach the apex of human perfection. Through an interchange of cycles and gyric phases, man gradually evolves into an integrated personality. Even cultural movements have to undergo change by alternation. At the end of one cycle, the world enters a new gyre and a different contradictory phase. Till man completes his partial mind, till he passes through

> Twenty-and-eight the phases of the moon,
> The full and the moon's dark and all the crescents,
> Twenty-and-eight, and yet but six-and-twenty
> The cradles that a man must needs be rocked in:
> For there's no human life at the full or the dark[45]

he must shudder in many cradles,

> Ravening through century after century,
> Ravening, raging, and uprooting that he may come
> Into the desolation of reality.[46]

Those who think that they have buried their man in the dust have only thrown him into the human mind again, into a new gyre. A man does not complete his self in a single existence. Man's two extremities— "of race and that of soul"—extend over many phasic lifetimes:

From marble of a broken sepulchre,
Or dark betwixt the polecat and the owl,
Or any rich, dark nothing disinter
The workman, noble and saint, and all things run
On that unfashionable gyre again.[47]

The humble and the wise do not "break down and weep" when they see the desolate face of reality. They know that day brings round the night, that before dawn man's glory and his monuments are gone:

All things fall and are built again,
And those that build them again are gay.[48]

We "begin to live when we have conceived life as a tragedy,"[49] says Yeats. The poet as Hero goes on singing in ecstasy even as the last darkness begins to close upon him. It is tragic gaiety transfiguring all the dread and heroically mocking defeat. Man's life may be determined but he has, at least, the freedom to defy. The poet as contemplative man is the antithesis of the man of action but his dreams have the potency to defeat the actual at every point.

In *Essays and Introductions,* Yeats explains how even at the point of defeat the hero does not succumb. He does not permit the tragic to overwhelm the strangely passionate and heroic moment of experience. The tragic hero dramatizes in himself not only his own, but the fate of all men. His tragedy is, therefore, more than equal that of other men before him. Since Yeats's imagination is alive only when, as Donoghue says, the theme is "race" or "kindred" and "honey of generation,"[50] it responds only to life that has reached a certain intensity of definition. Only special and heightened moments matter. Like Timon of Athens who contemplates his own end and orders his tomb, and Cleopatra who sets the asps to her bosom, the hero's agony is for "all men's fate":

> That shaping joy has kept the sorrow pure, as it had kept it were the emotion love or hate, for the nobleness of the arts is in the mingling of contraries, the extremity of sorrow, the extremity of joy, perfection of personality, the perfection of its surrender.[51]

Though Yeats's *A Vision*--his only philosophical book—has given rise to controversial views and counter-arguments, it does have a bearing on his poetical theory. It forms a necessary part of the total system in which he chose to work, not only perfecting the art but also the life. The book is born of the romanticist's need to evolve a system of thought that would contain within it all his ideas about man, civilization and history, and also support a personality that can endure the contradictions without annihilating them. In other words, Yeats needed this greater "dharma"[52] in which to pursue his unique poetic "swadharma." Only in the context of this larger structure could he, he thought, find a pretext for a whole lifetime's struggle toward Unity of Being.

In his belief that man can attain a fuller realization of himself through art, Yeats has given to poetry a high destiny. Unlike rhetoric, which arises from a quarrel with others, poetry is made out of a quarrel with ourselves. In Yeats's poetry, "the self as a feeling subject with the self as an object" are submitted to the observation of the world. But "the poem is something more than the depiction of both these selves or part-selves." It is "a fuller statement by a fuller self of the conditions of life, and the selves that appear in the poetry are instrumental to the framing of such a statement."[53] The poem contains within it the varying shades and moods of life. Its complexity is partly achieved by a struggle and tension that is only temporarily resolved.

Interestingly, the struggle itself was always more valuable and important, for Yeats, than the final reconciliation. "Realization," "fulfilment" and "end" are for the practical men of the world. For the artist pledged to his art, there is greater power and glory in the quest or pilgrimage undertaken than the end of the journey. To keep the search on, to artistically renew life—which provides raw material for art—and to be able to re-enter the arena of life again and again, the poet must retain enough poetic energy to continue the dynamic interplay of polar forces. For the "next" poem to be made, a fresh contest, drawing its sustenance from previous, partial resolutions, may be enacted. In this way, Yeats knew, one would never cease to be a Poet or Hero.

NOTES

1. W.B. Yeats, *Uncollected Prose,* collected and edited by John P. Frayne and Colten Johnson, Vol.II, Reviews, Articles and other miscellaneous prose 1897-1939 (London: Macmillan, 1975), p. 370.
2. *W.B. Yeats Self-Critic: A Study of His Early Verse and the Later Poetry,* II Volumes in One (Berkeley: Univ. of California Press, 1971), p. vii.
3. Erich Heller, *The Disinherited Mind: Essays in Modern German Literature and Thought,* p. 153.
4. T.S. Eliot, "Yeats," *Selected Prose,* ed. John Hayward, p. 199.
5. Cited from Richard Ellmann, *Yeats: The Man and the Masks* (1949; rpt. London: Faber and Faber, 1969), p. 54.
6. Katharine Tynan, from "Twenty-five Years: Reminiscences," 1913, in *W.B. Yeats: The Critical Heritage,* ed. A. Norman Jeffares (London: Routledge and Kegan Paul, 1977), p. 181.
7. Cited from *The Modern Tradition: Backgrounds of Modern Literature,* ed. Richard Ellmann and Charles Feidelson (New York: Oxford Univ. Press, 1965), p. 170.
8. Yeats, *Selected Criticism and Prose,* ed. A. Norman Jeffares (1964, London: Pan Books, 1980), p. 171.
9. Cited from *The Modern Tradition,* p. 170.
10. Cited from Richard Ellmann, *Man and the Masks,* p. 5.
11. Yeats, "Poetry and Tradition," *Selected Criticism and Prose,* p. 162.
12. *Ibid.,* "The Symbolism of Poetry," p. 46.

13. Cited from Richard Ellmann, *Man and the Masks*, pp. 188-89.
14. Yeats, "The Second Coming," *CP*, pp. 210-11.
15. Cited from Richard Ellmann, *Man and the Masks*, p. 278.
16. Yeats, *Selected Criticism and Prose*, p. 266.
17. *Ibid.*, p. 255
18. "Tragic Generation," *Autobiographies*, p. 332
19. Yeats, "Adam's Curse," *CP*, pp. 88-89.
20. W.B. Yeats, "The Cutting of an Agate," *Essays and Introductions* (1961; rpt. London: Macmillan, 1971), p. 271.
21. Herbert Read, *The Tenth Muse: Essays in Criticism* (London: Routledge and Kegan Paul, 1957), p. 207.
22. *Ibid.*
23. Yeats, *Autobiographies*, p. 469.
24. *Ibid.*, p. 87.
25. *Selected Criticism and Prose*, p. 164.
26. Cited From Richard Ellmann, *Man and the Masks*, pp. 285-86.
27. Cited from Richard Ellmann, *The Identity of Yeats* (London: Macmillan, 1954), p. 8.
28. William Blake, "The Marriage of Heaven and Hell," *Blake's Poems and Prophesies*, ed. Max Plowman (1927; rpt. London: Dent, 1970), p. 43.
29. "Collective Intellect: Yeats, Synge and Nietzsche," *Essays and Studies*, 1973, p. 87.
30. Yeats, *Autobiographies*, p. 470.
31. *Selected Criticism and Prose*, p. 173.
32. *Ibid.*
33. "Ego Dominus Tuus," *CP*, p. 182.
34. *Ibid.*, p. 181.
35. Matthew 10:39.
36. *Selected Criticism and Prose*, p. 167.
37. *Ibid.*
38. *Ibid.*
39. *Ibid.*, p. 169
40. "Ego Dominus Tuus," *CP*, p. 182.
41. Giorgio Melchiori, *The Whole Mystery of Art: Pattern into Poetry in the Work of W.B. Yeats* (London: Routledge and Kegan Paul, 1960), p. 173.
42. Yeats, *A Vision* (1937; London: Papermac, 1981), p. 193.
43. *Selected Criticism and Prose*, p. 255.
44. *Ibid.*, p. 179.

45. *CP*, pp. 184-85.
46. *Ibid.*, "Meru," p. 333.
47. *Ibid.*, "The Gyres," p. 337.
48. *Ibid.*, "Lapis Lazuli," p. 339.
49. Yeats, *Autobiographies*, p. 189.
50. *Yeats* (1971; rpt. Glasgow: Fontana, 1982), p. 29.
51. *Selected Criticism and Prose*, p. 164.
52. Refer Chapter I, note 9.
53. George T. Wright, *The Poet in the Poem: The Personae of Eliot, Yeats, and Pound* (New York: Gordian Press, 1974), p. 122.

Unity: The Aesthetic of Irony

Yeats counted himself as one of "a species of man" for whom "nothing so much matters as Unity of Being." But if he sought it "as Goethe sought, who was not of that species, I but combine in myself, and perhaps as it now seems, looking backward, in others also, incompatibles." Whereas "Goethe, in whom objectivity and subjectivity were intermixed . . . as the dark is mixed with the light at the eighteenth Lunar Phase," attempted to understand it, as Wilhelm Meister did, "intellectually, critically, and through a multitude of deliberately chosen experiences; events and forms of skill gathered as if for a Collector's Cabinet," Yeats was looking for the kind of Unity of Being "where all the nature murmurs in response if but a single note be touched." It was a Unity "found emotionally, instinctively, by the rejection of all experience not of the right quality, and by the limitation of its quantity."[1]

Yeats used the term "Unity of Being" as Dante did when he compared beauty in the *Convito* to a "perfectly proportioned human body."[2] His father from whom he learned the term preferred to compare it to a "musical instrument so strung that if we touch a string all the strings murmur faintly."[3] Every response must affect, even disturb, that delicately-held unity.

Yeats's father, a careful observer of his son's progress, insisted that "the wild spirit of your imagination" should have been "wedded to concrete fact" and "the game of life" made its subject because poetry is that which is "in closest and most intimate union with the positive realities and complexities of life."[4] For one whose aim is to achieve Unity of Being, the modern preference for intellect over imagination cannot be desirable. It is not surprising that in an attempt to regain a unified sensibility "poets tried again to be concrete," as Kermode notes, and "to charge their thinking with passion, to restore to poetry a truth independent of the presumptuous intellect."[5] Yeats says in the *Autobiographies* that his father thought Dowden believed too much in the intellect, whereas "all valuable education was but a stirring up of the emotions."[6] "In the completely emotional man," J.B. Yeats wrote, "the least awakening of feeling is a harmony in which every chord of every feeling vibrates."[7]

Personally, Yeats considered his Christ "a legitimate deduction from the Creed of St. Patrick," equivalent to "that Unity of Being Dante compared to a perfectly proportioned human body, Blake's 'Imagination', what the Upanishads have named 'Self': nor is this unity distant and therefore intellectually understandable."[8] It has to be emotionally, instinctively or intuitively apprehended.

By linking the attainment of Unity of Being with "Personality," Yeats made a further advance: It is possible to attain Unity, but not for all. There are "men who cannot possess 'Unity of Being,' who must not seek it or express it—and who, so far from seeking an anti-self, a Mask that delineates a being in all things, the opposite to their natural state can but seek the suppression of the anti-self, till the natural state alone remains."[9] Such men, in being unable to conceive of the anti-self, are denied this unity. Only he who is able to accept the "dark brother" within can realize it. Yeats wrote in *Anima Hominis* that "the other self, the anti-self or the antithetical self, as one may choose to name it, comes but to those who are no longer deceived, whose passion is reality."[10]

Looking back upon the self he embodied in his writing, Yeats found most pleasure in "those verses where it seems to me I have found something hard and cold, some articulation of the Image which is the opposite of all that I am in my daily life."[11] The quest for Unity was, in Yeats's case, closely interlinked with the perfection of his art. All the "incompatibles" were to be combined, and art reflected this by a unity of perception.

Any unity which does not comprehend a dialectical tension, arising from an interaction of diametrically opposed entities, is a unity that lacks strength and productive power. A theory of unity without diversity is either totally irrelevant or too fundamental to be dealt with. It is a naive mind that would accept a simple unity which does not hold against the complexity of experience.

Yeats wanted Unity of Being to be the crowning achievement of life but he knew his aspiration was impossible to realize without a corresponding Unity of Culture which is constituted by the ability of an integrated self to direct every part of the whole toward a unified development. The mature Yeats realized "how little that Unity, however wisely sought, is possible without a Unity of Culture in class or people that is no longer possible at all."[12] According to Yeats, "the enemy of this unity was abstraction, meaning by abstraction not the distinction but the isolation of occupation, or class or faculty."[13]

It is possible to show that these ideas of Yeats regarding Culture and Self have historical and philosophical basis, and are endorsed by studies carried out, in recent times, in the field of psychoanalysis to find the deeper roots of human culture. For example, if, in the Middle Ages, unity of culture was largely present, it was because, as Mason explains, the distinction between classes was not so sharp as to permit their isolation. Like Yeats's, Mumford's vision of culture, while it takes into account the integrated self, makes both the self and a possible unity of culture reciprocal. Mumford argues that only in the acceptance of the whole self of man lies the future of a unified culture:

> Unified man must accept the id without giving it primacy: he must foster the superego, without making it depress the energies it needs for its own fuller expression.[14]

If primitive man was relatively whole, it was because, in transcending his animal state, he left the real world behind. The idea of "otherness" did not exist for him. His reactions to the external world, says Mumford, were chiefly based on self-projections. With the dawn of civilization, this subjectivity was sought to be curbed by exacting obedience to powers outside himself—gods and kings. In making man recognize the limitations of his own nature, civilization helped to give him a sense of reality. However,

> in recognizing as absolute claims outside the self, civilized man ceased to live in a unified world: the fragmentary man, with his split and contradictory selves, came into existence.[15]

In a desperate and determined attempt to regain wholeness, the schism was further widened, separating the inner and the outer man. When value was placed on the subjective, man grew in outrageous self-importance even as civilization reduced him to a nonentity.

No matter how well we fortify the barriers between the two worlds, each is constantly breaking through and trying to penetrate the other, demanding a larger unfolding. Perhaps what man needs is "a fuller exposure to sunlight above ground and a richer soil in the unconscious,"[16] says Mumford. Yeats believed that "revelation is from the self, but from that age-long memorized self, that shapes the elaborate shell of the mollusc and the child in the womb, that teaches the birds to make their nest; and that genius is a crisis that joins the buried self for certain moments to our trivial daily mind."[17]

Fritjof Capra[18] rightly points out that a study of the history of civilization shows a recurrent pattern in cultural growth related to processes of fluctuation and relative stability. This dual movement comprises the fundamental dynamics of the Universe. Numerous philosophers of modern times endorse the interplay between polar forces as a fundamental rhythm of the universe. Saint-Simon sees in the history of civilizations a series of alternating periods: the organic and the critical. Herbert Spencer calls it integrations and differentiations. Hegel refers to a spiral human development from a phase of unity to disunity, followed by re-integration at a higher plane.

For various reasons, the ideal of wholeness which was held high by the best of men has been present in the culture of man only for transitory phases like the Greek flowering of the fifth and fourth centuries B.C., and the European Renaissance. Yeats placed the ideal period to "Somewhere about 1450, though later in some parts of Europe by a hundred years or so, and in some earlier" when men "attained to personality in great numbers, 'Unity of Being,' and became like 'a perfectly proportioned human body,' and as men so fashioned held places of power, their nations had it too, prince and ploughman sharing that thought and feeling. What afterwards showed for rifts and cracks were there already, but imperious impulse held all together."[19]

Though attempts have been made to formulate a philosophy of life and of living, keeping in perspective the needs and requirements of a unity of culture that may contribute to unity of being, the basic limitation has been, as Mumford and others point out, to interpret the complex in terms of the simple, the higher in terms of the lower—the primary drawback of the technique of reductive logic used by the conventional sciences. Philosophy is now turning to a theory of the organic development of the person that aims at enhancing every department of thought and perception by interaction and integration. The preoccupation with unity suggests that as an expression of the manifold facets of man's personality, human culture has been aspiring, right from the beginning, for a total and unified development that comprehends a diversity of interests without neglecting any.

Progress in the S-matrix theory and Bell's theorem in Modern Physics has brought in the notion of order, basic unity or fundamental inter-relatedness as a key element in our understanding of reality. Leaving the Cartesian view behind, physicists are leading us to a holistic and intrinsically dynamic conception of the universe. The fundamental theory of natural evolution has gone beyond the mechanistic model held by Newton. Darwin's Evolutionary Theory, and the latest findings in electrodynamics clearly indicate that the universe is more complex than Descartes and Newton made it out to be. Even thought arises by virtue of the undifferentiated existence suddenly acquiring a break in its unity. If the realm of dream or the Unconscious is higher than the realm of thought or the Conscious, it is because in it we find all realizations present as potentialities and, therefore, as unities. All potentialities are unities, actual realizations are not. Correspondingly, the dipolarity and dynamic nature of life can be defined and explained only against a potential unity. A notion of pure unity that does not comprehend interconnectedness and continual alternating integrations and differentiations is too fundamental to have any practical, operative value.

In Aesthetics, the concept of unity may be traced back to the earliest times—to Plato who was the first among Western thinkers to propose an artistic doctrine of unity. He suggested, in connection with the musical scales, that unity is a reconciliation of opposites. After him, Horace conceived of a unity of effect achieved by a careful ordering and arrangement. He made it analogous to music and painting in terms of a harmonious blending of colours, light, etc. Longinus derived it from an intensity of feeling that would artistically reconcile opposing elements by a process of selection.[20]

In the seventeenth century, before science and the "new Philosophy" called all in doubt and a dissociation of sensibility set in, the metaphysicals, as Johnson remarked of them, "yoked the most heterogeneous ideas by violence together." Theirs was a logical and intellectual unity, not an intuitive one. By saying that the ideas were "yoked by violence together," Johnson stressed on how difficult it was to bring about the conjunction. Something went wrong in the late seventeenth century in our thinking and apprehension that resulted in a loss of centritude. Eliot said:

> It is something which had happened to the mind of England between the time of Donne or Lord Herbert of Cherbury and the time of Tennyson and Browning; it is the difference between the intellectual poet and the reflective poet. Tennyson and Browning are poets, and they think; but they do not feel their thought as immediately as the odour of a rose.[21]

Yeats believed the

> mischief began at the end of the seventeenth century when man became passive before a mechanized nature.[22]

If, as discussed earlier, primitive man had been able to sustain the relative wholeness of his vision, what had helped him was a departure from the real world. His reactions to the external world were based on self-projections. When we look at the pre-Copernican or Ptolemaic period, we find man living in a naive assumption that he is the centre of the universe. The old metaphysics also led him to believe so, and the classical notion of order persisted, sustaining his simple dream of unity till we come to the modern, post-Copernican era.

The increasing insecurity begins to show itself in the confusing work of Dr. Johnson who, as Krieger explains, though naggingly aware of the threats to his dream of neoclassical order, continued to hold on to his classic vision. There was a consolidated attempt to fortify the rationalists's assumption of the objectivity of the world. Until the eighteenth century, man was fairly confident that the world was well-ordered and made for man. Hume's contention that reality as we see it is an illusion, and Kant's that our mind is in a position to constitute the structures by which it lives shattered this complacency. Kant, the philosophical Copernicus, made the perceiving "I" all-important because he gave to the mind the power to constitute the categories of reality.

"Philosophy in Yeats's unofficial sense, endorsed by his version of Symbolism and the *anima mundi,* enabled him to think," Donoghue says, "of the world as sacred; like Swedenborg's 'desolate places,' animated by spirits."[23] For Yeats, the "great enemy" was Locke. He resented what he thought was Locke's separation of the primary and secondary qualities. "Descartes, Locke, and Newton," he said, "took away the world and gave us its excrement instead."[24] Yeats found it unfortunate that "the conception of a physical world without colour, sound, taste, tangibility, though indicted by Berkeley . . . has remained the assumption of science, the groundwork of every text-book."[25] Berkeley restored the world by bringing back to us "the world that only exists because it shines and sounds."[26] And, by doing so, Berkeley liberated the power of the imaginative perception. The question as to whether the sacredness of nature is innate or imposed and derivative did not bother Yeats. For him, "it was enough for holiness if a thing was related to man."[27] Even God had to be assimilated to the human world. Inasmuch as man was creator/actor in the world of his Imagination, the creative joy made him almost Godlike—distant from man.

> Death and life were not
> Till man made up the whole,
> Made lock, stock and barrel
> Out of his bitter soul.[28]

The eighteenth-century cosmic-aesthetic structure depended, Krieger explains, on a spatial imagination which could freeze all flux into unchanging universes where time is not. This view, however, belongs to a "naive realism" since all along, with or without the Kantian imperative, we ought to have seen that the easy convenient metaphors our spatial imagination invented to substitute the flowing metaphors which elude our rational need for the boundaries making for entityhood cannot be relied upon. What brought the almost dogmatic belief in a well-ordered universe was the anthropomorphic view that the objective order existed as a reflection of the rational order of the mind. As against such a feeling of security, there was the hidden fear that perhaps our claims to objective order were merely mental constructs or projections of man's need for order. If the Kantian alternative pushed the choice on to the subject and insisted on the mind's power to impose order, it still did not remove the sense of insecurity. There was the metaphysical claim of the realist, on the one hand, that the mind is tailor-made for the universe and, on the other, the critical idealist's view that the universe is tailor-made for the mind.[29]

In the later part of the eighteenth-century a major disruption took place which found man ejected from his universe. It was a fall akin to the loss of Eden and a loss of confidence. Man felt keenly the "existential loneliness of his exile," and began to look for a justifiable substitute for the objective reality which had slipped from him. On the one hand he remained helplessly outside and on the other, alone inside himself, still an outsider. As an isolated subject, the only choice that remained was to master himself and to create an "egotistical sublime," his uniquely human world. Inasmuch as it gave him a world of freedom, it was a fortunate fall. He continued to long for the lost unity. But it was no longer the poet's naive and simple, "sensuous unity." It was a higher "moral unity." Nature which provides the only unity available to his senses or racial memory—Yeats's: Have not all races had their first unity from a mythology that marries them to rock and hill?[30]—served as a metaphor of the unity that may be embodied in the world of ideas. As a metaphor infused with moral attributes by man, Nature became a sympathetic spectator, if not a participant, giving rise to the "pathetic fallacy."

The early nineteenth-century writers sought to turn all this to positive advantage. The romantic conception of the possibilities inherent in the subject and the poetic imagination gathered new and enlarged meanings. The cartesian dichotomy resulted in a disjunction between the spiritual and the material world, a disjunction that manifested itself in the twentieth century in the distinction between minority culture and mass civilization—Yeats's fear that we are perhaps "approaching a supreme moment of self-consciousness, the two halves of the soul separate and face to face."[31] The romantic poet sought to bring the dichotomy together into an organic unity in terms of a Unity of Feeling, Unity as Vision of an immanent God in Nature, Unity achieved by mediation of the imagination acting in its capacity as a symbol-making faculty and, above all, Unity as the imagination's repetition, in the finite mind of the poet, of the eternal act of creation in the infinite I AM.

The romantics saw nature, man and all things in their related antithesis. From monopolarity they moved towards dipolarity. The neoclassical writers and the philosophy of the Enlightenment had entertained an essentially monopolar view. Though it is true that the absence of a consistent rationalist point of view is responsible, Krieger observes, for Pope's "inward failure of confidence in the power of his own spatial imagination" or the spatial imagination of his time to freeze the temporal resistances into a pattern, there may perhaps be another factor involved. Pope and Johnson tried to pair contraries into a balance but the shortcoming was that they made a specific choice, deciding which member of the pair was desirable. Unlike the neoclassical writers, the romantics resisted the making of choices. Their way of looking at things was essentially dipolar. Applying the Coleridgean ideal of reconciliation, they converted the "either-or" to an "either and or" way of perception. By balancing sameness with difference in a productive unity, they kept both sides together and yet apart.

The recurrent question we are confronted with is whether the unity that we perceive is a fabrication of our mind. Is it self-imposed because we are genetically programmed to prefer order? Each age is equidistant from Arcadia and perhaps man in all ages feels nostalgic about a time when Unity persisted without perpetually threatening to break apart. One thing is true—that a return to unity, order and Eden, however illusionary, has become a dire necessity for modern man living alone in a crowded world. Without this Dream he cannot uphold either the wholeness of personal vision (Swadharma/Personal Integrity) or the cultural identity (Kaladharma/Time Spirit) of civilization. Like Tiresias, the central mythical figure of *The Waste Land,* he is torn between what he carries within him as personal guilt, and the total guilt of mankind. Failing to regain the lost paradisal unity, he may attempt to create a new centre, a virtual axis if not a real one, to support the structure of reality. In a "rage for order" he may launch a vehement protest against all limitations put upon reality. Yeats declared in frenzied range:

> I mock Plotinus' thought
> And cry in Plato's teeth,
> Death and life were not
> Till man made up the whole
> Made lock, stock and barrel
> Out of his bitter soul,
> Aye, sun and moon and star, all.[32]

Since "man's life is thought," he cannot, despite his terror, cease "ravening, raging, and uprooting" that he may come into the "desolation of reality."[33]

Eliot, in reading the history of English poetry using referential terms like "unified sensibility" and "dissociation of sensibility," linked what had happened to poetry to a cultural crisis, that is, to the problem of existence and the individual. A loss of certitude can pose a threat to the artistic enterprise. Yeats thought "there could be no aim for poet or artist except expression of a 'Unity of Being' like that of a 'perfectly proportioned human body'."[34] Would it be possible to exploit the causes of the loss of unity and convert them into a positive force to forge the connections once again? Though Yeats accepted that it is the totalitarian mind that has given allowance to an impositional unity, a pathetically human acceptance of the reality of illusion, he also felt that heroism lies in the poet's attempt to create meaning out of apparent disorder— "dream and so create," "out of poet's imaginings"—

> All those things whereof
> Man makes a superhuman
> Mirror-resembling dream.[35]

The poet's "dreams shall have the potency to effect the actual at every point."[36]

Though the power of the word has been subverted in our times, Whitehead would concede that the minimal order we live by is the order of words. Without time and space, no experience can be had, and verbalization as a specialization of time might still give a fairly adequate representation of the fluidity of human experience. As a result, there is the new critical need to shift the emphasis on the autonomous nature of a work of art, to a poetic world embodying the thesis and antithesis within Nature and human nature in the unity of its form.

The concept of unity, both as a critical criterion and as a method of exposition, has become more important at the formalistic, psychological and mythical levels of criticism in the last two decades during which a number of apparently different theories of unity have been set forth—by Richards as a reconciliation of impulsus, by Cleanth Brooks as a balance of thought and feeling in terms of an interaction of theme with language and metaphor, by the surrealists as a unification of the mind by freeing the unconscious, by the Freudians through dream-pattern and free association, by Jung through individuation, Gestalt and the use of archetypal myth-motifs. Lawrence enunciated the profound and sensitive responsibility of the individual. Eliot sought it through a return to Christian tradition and literary anthropology, and Yeats by turning everything around him—friends, politics, religion, Irish folklore—into a legend or personal mythology.

Can the artistic form be an adequate mode of expression of the intuitive experience of the artist? Read's answer would be:

> In the biological world form is related to function—to the process of growth. In art the function of form is symbolic: Form is a perceptible symbol for a particular state of mind.[37]

It is not possible to reconcile the spiritual and the corporeal logically since each is the opposite of the other. But what is logically impossible may, as Benoit says, be symbologically achieved. The polar opposites exist by virtue of and at the expense of each other. They are mutually generative:

> Each polarity, while being a duality from its own point of view, remains nevertheless a unity. Thus, while, *qua* duality, it has already been polarized, yet *qua* unity, it may again be polarized into two further contraries, and so ad infinitum.[38]

This is a polarity that underlies all things. By defining life as the "power which discloses itself from within as a principle of unity in the many" or as "the principle of individuation," Coleridge explained the "tendency to progressive individuation by means of polarity." This is the "central idea of his cosmology, applying as it does not only to the whole of the phenomenal world, but to the noumenal also." [39]

The organic unity of a work of art is not passive or static. It embodies the dynamic quality of life itself. It gives aesthetic form to our emotions by re-enacting the fullness of experience by means of a complexity of context that takes into account the continual oscillation between opposing poles. It is this kind of poetic integration that we find in much of the later poetry of Yeats. The polarity is of productive unity. Coleridge calls it "separative projection" or a "tendency at once to individuate and to connect, to detach but so as either to retain or reproduce attachment." In Nature, too, there is the same "separative projection." While it strives to detach from itself what is similar to itself, it struggles in the same act to overcome that detachment, thereby maintaining unity. Coleridge's theory of the imagination as the "living Power and prime Agent of all human Perception, and as a repetition in the finite mind of the eternal act of creation in the infinite I Am,"[40] conceives the imagination not merely in its characteristic power to create but also as a unifying principle. In the *Biographia Literaria*, Coleridge explains the role of the poet. He is the one who, in ideal perfection, brings

> the whole soul of man into activity, with the subordination of its faculties to each other, according to their relative worth and dignity. He diffuses a tone and spirit of unity that blends and (as it were) fuses, each into each, by that synthetic and magical power to which we have exclusively appropriated the name of imagination. This power . . . reveals itself in the balance or reconciliation of opposite or discordant qualities.[41]

The imagination is a shaping and modifying power that "dissolves, diffuses, dissipates, in order to re-create; or where this process is rendered impossible, yet still, at all events, struggles to idealize and to unify."[42] Even as it brings together, it gives rise to a tension that breaks into duality, only to re-unify once again.

When the productive unity involves itself in the double act of reproducing as well as separating itself by a kind of dialectical thesis and antithesis, the unity it maintains becomes one of interchange. Yeats's poetry of dialogue, wherein the persona speaks from two poles of his being, seeks to capture the complexity and completeness of experience, and re-establish the intimate connections that art has with life. If the mature Yeats chose not to escape into an Isle of Bliss, it was because the world of unalloyed gaiety became limited and inadequate. The legendary heroes that were objective personifications of subjective experience and conflict proved dissatisfying. He needed a more powerful mode of expression that would bring together different voices and centre them in a single poem. *A Dialogue of Self and Soul* and *Ego Dominus Tuus* are illustrative of this type of poetry.

The question is—Can poetry of this kind be spontaneous? Would it not involve too deliberate and definite an act of Will to be poetry at all? The greatest poetry may be a spontaneous outburst. But it was Coleridge's belief that spontaneity gets its impulse from a productive tension with the Will which invigorates the imagination to shape and modify all the elements in a poem or a work of art into a unified effect. As Abrams explains, "inclusiveness" became the criterion of poetic excellence:

> the co-existence in a poem of "opposite or discordant qualities," provided that, these have been blended or "reconciled" into unity by the synthetic power which Coleridge attributes to the imagination. . . . It is merely the application in the province of aesthetics of the generative principle which underlies Coleridge's metaphysical system in its totality.[43]

While the poem may contain within it a number of images and symbols, the poem itself may be a symbol, relating the parts to the whole and the whole to the parts. The individual work of art becomes a dialectical structure conceiving in its own multiplicity the unity of its form. According to Coleridge, a poet's heart and intellect must be unified with the great appearances of nature. In projecting his inmost being into the appearances of nature lies the unique insight of the artist. And, the condition of the union of the artist's being with nature is passion in the poet. Passion is the formative power of the poem. It is "the straining of man's being" against what "obstructs its unity."[44]

Balance and reconciliation was the crux of Coleridge's theory, and the nineteenth-century writers went to it for help when they found they were confused by the rational separation between the material and the spiritual. The symbol cemented the division between the image and idea, the concrete and abstract, while the difference between them was, nevertheless, maintained. The poem as symbol encompassed multiplicity in its unity. In view of the uses to which the Coleridgean imagination was put, it is not surprising that our time "is busily returning to his view of the imagination as the symbol-making faculty because the problem of disjunction in all its forms is so much our own."[45]

Richards comes close to the Coleridgean concept of the imagination in his *Principles of Literary Criticism.* He makes a distinction between two types of poetry, the exclusive and the inclusive—the poetry which excludes the opposite and discordant qualities of an experience from the poem, and poetry of the inclusive kind which resolves the discord via the imagination to achieve a larger unity. Richards's poetry of inclusion is, as Brooks says,

> richer, more complicated, and more thoroughly detached from local issues and actions. Because of the nature of language it appears more interesting, and because of the nature of human experience, more honest.[46]

It is not difficult to see among the new critics the same principle looming large, though in the background, and being used as a critical criterion for judging the success of a poem. Eliot talking of unified sensibility and looking forward to bringing thought and feeling together as a single experience, and Richards speaking of the unity of a single response comprising the total effect of all the formal elements within the poem seem to point to the same idea though they employ different terminology. While Tate gives his critical assent to a poem in terms of a unity of the furthest extremes of extension and intention, Yvor Winters argues for the unity of the extremes of denotation and connotation.

A poetry that appeals to only one set of impulses would be "partisan." On the other hand, by making present a number of different impulses, poetry would not only organize impulse, it would bring the "whole soul of man into activity." For Richards, the answer is in

> irony, which will allow opposing impulses to be aroused simultaneously.[47]

This is not the irony of "simple inversion." Richards's conception of irony seems to "demand that the poem, while stating one view . . . should by ambiguity or some other device present the opposite view at the same time."[48] It relates closely to "irony" in Schlegel's sense of the term which, as Paz defines it, is "love for the contradiction which lives in each of us, and awareness of this contradiction." Irony, that great invention of the Romantics, says Paz, reveals "the duality of what seemed whole, the split in what is identical, the other side of reason; it is the disruption of the principle of identity."[49] It shields the artist from the accusation that the unified vision has been too easily attained.

Yeats's *Sailing to Byzantium* embodies this ironic attitude. Though the speaker has undertaken a journey away from a country which is not for old men, he talks, in the first stanza, of "that country" with a vehemence that betrays a hidden bitterness because it no longer belongs to him. And this is captured, with a kind of poignancy, in the resultant irony of the last two lines:

> Caught in that sensual music all neglect
> Monuments of unaging intellect.[50]

If we go by Brooks's justification of the ironic mode in its ability to handle with greater fairness the complex nature of reality, I would suggest that *Sailing to Byzantium* shows not the difficulty or to present a single aspect of reality, he would be simplifying the depth and complexity of human experience. Without irony the poetic context would become bare and simplistic. Therefore, reacting to this problem, Cleanth Brooks and Robert Penn Warren make irony a standard or device, a principle of structure, or even a strategy, by which to remain invulnerable against attack. Warren clarifies:

> the poet wishes to indicate that his vision has been earned, that it can survive reference to the complexities and contradictions of experience. And irony is one such device of reference.[51]

These explanations show how many of the arguments of the modern theorists of poetry and art actually draw their essence from Coleridge though the debt remains unacknowledged, even denied. What appears in Coleridge as unity of effect when the imagination "draws intimations of an ultimate unity from immediate severances and divisions not by excluding the different forces but by accommodating them,"[52] is seen in Richards as "the resolution of a welter of disconnected impulses into a single ordered response."[53]

The question is whether we are to regard "unity" as merely a formal affair. Even if it is validated by an authentic transformation from within, how are we to actually penetrate the poem/persona and reach the person?

There are, primarily, two kinds of unity—Coleridge's unity—as being found in the genesis of the mind of the poet who in ideal perfection brings the whole soul of man into activity, and the metaphysical unity involving, as it did in the case of Donne, Marvell and others, a certain amount of "willing." While Coleridge's unity inheres in the mind of the poet, the metaphysical one is more verbal and semantic, and is embodied at the imagistic level. Though modern critical protestantism borrows from the romantic concept of unity, it has more affinity with unity-as idea—the formal unity of the metaphysical—than to unity-as being of the romanticists. In their professed attempt to banish all external reference— "it is never what a poem says that matters, but what it is"—the New Critics have tried to shift the locus of balance from the poet to the poem. Is unity or formal resolution a genetic compulsion or a dramatic necessity? Is it a critical delusion? Are we using unity as an alibi to enable us to write a more meaningful poetry? Is the unity felt more in its absence than in its presence? We have to accept that even when we are watching for "conflict" and "interaction" our mind is centred on unity by indirection. It is only in terms of its opposite that we can define unity, and vice versa.

It is necessary to understand what kind of machinery a poet uses or adopts to make his meaning out of the existing chaos of experience. While Eliot reacted to the disappearance of God in nature by turning to ancient myth, to literary culture and oriental philosophy before seeking refuge in Christianity, Yeats found his answer to the withdrawal of Pan and the loss of the magical view in the invention of his own "Arcady" where Pan is replaced by Man. Yeats veered away from Symbolism to Irish oral tradition because, haunted by ancestral voices and witness to things falling apart, Yeats's fertile muse invented, made and remade a protean self whose strength would validate the sustaining meaning of each poem. Donoghue puts it well in *The Ordinary Universe:*

> An oral culture commits itself to the human situation in a sense that symbolism tried to evade. It assumes the integrity of the Person and the validity of temporal life: It has no interest in the inscrutable Silence of Symbolism. What Yeats missed in modern literature, besides 'excess' was 'emotion of multitude'.[54]

Whereas tradition, for Eliot, was a "visual" field upon which the great works of the past figure as monuments, Yeats looked upon tradition as "voice" or a "choir of voices in which the new voice is heard." Dylan Thomas declared: Man, be my metaphor. Yeats said, "Myself must I remake," and put man at the centre. On finding that

> The woods of Arcady are dead,

And over is their antique joy;
Of old the world on dreaming fed;
Grey Truth is now her painted toy;[55]

he resorted to "words" because

Words alone are certain good.

Though superficially Yeats sought refuge in "words," he did not approve of a merely formal, verbal unity on the "semantic surface." He was not content to stop at unity-as idea, a unity that is merely stated. The poem may become a strategy by which to discover the possibilities within one's self. It can become a momentary stay against confusion, a kind of poetic eureka based on poetic vision. Unity would be suspect if merely stated. It must be dramatized in order to have the validity of earned vision.

As noted earlier, the artist's task is a hazardous one. The "earned" vision is difficult to embody. Also, the poet is apt to be mistaken for trying to communicate an egocentric experience even if he gives it the passionate reality of personal utterance. To shield himself, the modern writer makes use of irony to protect himself and the validity of what he conveys. Without the ironic mode, lyricism would be suspect and unacceptable.

Yeats's method was to exploit the ironic mode and make it an artistic device by which to fortify the self against attack. It could, at the same time, become a method by which to conceal the many fictions without their appearing fictitious. One would never be discovered even if one played a number of roles. For the ironic mode Yeats chose conflict as his tool. However, conflict is not used as a merely rhetorical tactic. It is more than verbal. It is a double-edged tool, serving as a heuristic strategy by which to enter into the central meaning of the poem and bring out the complexities involved in choice-making. Conflict is exploited for its engendering power. The energy generated from the first pair of contraries starts a chain reaction and releases a new set of discordants in a long series. Even where the poet seeks a resolution, it is only provisional and temporary, not anything final. Choice is postponed in the interest of conflict. Sometimes the inability to make a specific choice, and its procrastination, itself becomes the subject of poetry:

> Yeats's conflicts of self and anti-self are corresponding attempts to give subjectivity grounds other than itself. The validity of Yeats's procedure is not at all undermined by the fact that both self and anti-self are in equal measure imaginative constructions: The poet is setting his imagination to do for its own sake what Richards, following Coleridge in this respect, has named as the special work of imagination, taking the risk of oppositions, tensions, contradictions, so that the unity at last achieved will be correspondingly and richly earned.[56]

By making conflict a catalyst, in the struggle between opposites,—"the Image which is the opposite of all that I am in my daily life,"[57] as in Dante, Keats and Synge—to engender fresh conflicts continually, Yeats made it a mode by which to reveal the complex nature of life. In addition to that, conflict would also help to order life by the pattern of a single dominant conflict. While the poem "through complexity, (it) reveals experience, through control it disdains the messiness of experience."[58]

To do this, the imagination is not obliged to vote for nature to provide the ideal conjunction of appearances, to "wait for the spark from heaven to fall." If it waits for the ideal conjunction to take place, it would be difficult to write at all, especially when the poet has not himself inherited from the past the tradition of "one aim, one desire." He has to earn it by deliberately creating or discovering a tradition of his own. The imagination may, therefore, provoke the appearances of nature by making an intelligent use of conflict so that "unity comes only when it has been earned."

To provoke nature and the world of appearances, instead of waiting for the ideal conjunction that would provide the ground for unity, is to put not only the self but also the poetic imagination at stake. But not to take risks at this crucial juncture would be to admit timidity in the face of challenge. Yeats as artist was dauntless. He was willing to make the plunge. An artist who finds within himself a tension between "dream" and "action" would feel also an impulse or urge from inside himself to resolve the tension. A unity achieved at the expense of either dream or action is a unity that would appear, in the ultimate analysis, more of a defeat than a triumph. Therefore, Yeats made the mere quest for unity so important that failure in it would be no less important. Unless the artist finds some way of momentarily terminating the pain of isolation by a resolution leading to a temporary equilibrium, the world being what it is, he would be threatened with immediate extinction. If the poet could achieve in the poem a temporary victory that would retain enough of tensional energy to propel a fresh conflict, the process could go on forever. Like the romanticists, Yeats found his answer in the Image. He was aware that without the "daily victory" of a unifying Image, he would cease to be a poet. He knew that if poetry is the Image, life must be tragic—but "we begin to live when we have conceived life as a tragedy." He was not willing to "walk out of his dream." There was the eager and staunch belief that his dreams would have the potency to defeat the actual at every point and, in defiance of the artist's fate, Kermode says, he simply extended the dream to include everything.[59]

The symbol-making faculty or the symbolic imagination would use Symbol to unite the dichotomies by a careful identification. It would proceed to do so through *analogy*—"the true religion of modern poetry"—moving from metaphor to symbol as we see in Yeats's culminating symbol of the Dancer and the Tree in *Among School Children.* Analogy believes in "correspondences between all beings and worlds" and "rhymes and alliterations, metaphors and metonymies" which are the "modes of operation in analogical thought." If irony is dissonance in the poem, modern poetry is "awareness of this dissonance within analogy."[60]

In undertaking the transition from the world of action to the world of ideas, time to the timeless moment of eternity, the symbolic imagination has to begin from the lowest rung of the ladder. Endowed with a gift for concrete experience, the symbolic artist has the power to start with the "common thing." As Tate, quoting Williams for confirmation in the poetic practice of Dante, writes:

> It was, however high the phrases . . . the common thing from which Dante always started, as it was certainly the greatest and most common to which he came His images were the natural inevitable images—the girl in the street, the people he knew, the language he learned as a child. In them the great diagrams were perceived; from them the great myths opened; by them he understands the final end.[61]

Blackmur also argues that the symbolic imagination aims at "bringing to significance, to order, the knowledge we have above and below the level of the mind," and it does this by making its chief mode one of "participation in the life common to all men at all times."[62]

The symbolic poet may ascend the heights. The way up is not denied to him. But unlike the "angelic imagination" which bypasses the common and has a direct access to the beatific vision, the "symbolic imagination" cannot, in Tate's terminology, have any direct apprehension of the spiritual. It needs a via media. It has to relate itself to the "body" with which it began. To be able to face the spiritual truth in its physical body needs an exceptional type of courage, Tate acknowledges, and only rare persons of genius can do it. It is like the experience of death. Yeats writes in *Estrangement* that the "knowledge of reality" is "a kind of death."[63]

The symbolic imagination finds not only the necessity to start with the "common thing" but a compulsion to return to it. As in the case of Dante, the symbolic poet sees the image of "man" in the centre of the triune circle. From the uncommon to return to the common and mundane— "a mound of refuse or the sweepings of a street"—in a cycle as it were, is the arduous task of the symbolic artist:

> The high order of the poetic insight that the final insight must

> elude us, is dramatic in the sense that its fullest image is an action in the shapes of the world: it does not reject, it includes; it sees not only with but through the natural world, to what may lie beyond it.[64]

In W.B. Yeats we have a poet whose efforts to achieve Unity of Being brought him in confrontation with the dilemma faced by the symbolic imagination. Even as he reaches the top, the symbolic artist must invariably return to the bottom:

> Now that my ladder's gone,
> I must lie down where all the ladders start,
> In the foul rag-and-bone shop of the heart.[65]

The idea is to relate at all times the polarities of interaction without which no unity can be meaningfully achieved. A perpetual tension has to be kept up. Unity achieved in this manner would, in Coleridge's sense, lead to knowledge of reality. As Tate put it, the symbolic artist as hero, in having to return to the "bottom," fails in the sense that "he will have to start over again when he steps out of the 'poem',"[66] and re-enact the "daily victory" once more. The failure is a human fallibility and is heroically acknowledged as such: "Its humility is witnessed by its modesty. It never begins at the top; it carries the bottom along with it, however high it may climb."[67] Graham Hough explains that Yeats wanted to ascend to heaven but carrying all his sensual baggage with him, and this may be true. Yeats is indeed in the tradition of the symbolic poet.

The symbolic imagination's every ascent is only temporary since it must continually return to the bottom, making it "tragic in sentiment, if not always in form."[68] But it would be wrong to suggest that Yeats ended where he began. No doubt he returned to the "foul rag-and-bone shop of the heart," to the bottom where "all the ladders start," but by then he has come full circle. We must remember that for Yeats there could be no real defeat in this struggle. He never permitted himself to be overpowered by despair. He conceived a "tragic gaiety" in it:

What matter if I live it all once more?

He is "content to live it all again/ And yet again," even if "it be life to pitch/ Into the frog-spawn of a blind man's ditch."[69] If returning to the bottom, living it all again in "another poem" and enacting the "victory" in another Image is the price one has to pay for ascending to the top, he is willing to pay it. He says in *Lapis Lazuli:*

All things fall and are built again,
And those that build them again are gay.[70]

The price may be high, but so is the reward—an "abundant recompense."

NOTES

1. "The Stirring of the Bones," *Autobiographies*, pp. 354-55.
2. *Ibid.*, p. 190.
3. *Ibid.*
4. *W.B. Yeats: A Critical Anthology*, ed. William H. Pritchard (Middlesex: Penguin Books, 1972), p. 80.
5. Frank Kermode, *Romantic Image* (1957; rpt. London: Routledge and Kegan Paul, 1966), p. 141.
6. Yeats, *Autobiographies*, p. 88.
7. *Ibid.*
8. *Selected Criticism and Prose*, p. 263.
9. Yeats, *Autobiographies*, p. 247.
10. *Selected Criticism and Prose*, p. 170.
11. Yeats, *Autobiographies*, p. 274.
12. *Ibid.*, p. 355.
13. *Ibid.*, p. 190.
14. Lewis Mumford, "World Culture," *Interpretations and Forecasts: 1922-1972: Studies in Literature, History, Biography, Technics and Contemporary Society* (London: Secker and Warburg, 1973), p. 444.
15. *Ibid.*, p. 449.

16. *Ibid.*. p. 451.
17. *Ibid.*, p. 272.
18. *The Turning Point: Science, Society and the Rising Culture* (1982; New York: Bantam Books, 1983), p. 28.
19. Yeats, *Autcbiographies*, p. 291.
20. "Unity" *Encyclopedia of Poetry and Poetics*, ed. Alex Prèminger (1965; rpt. Princeton: Princeton Univ. Press, 1966), pp. 880-81.
21. "Metaphysical Poets," *Selected Prose*, p. 117.
22. Cited from *W.B. Yeats: A Critical Anthology*, p. 187.
23. Denis Donoghue, *Yeats*, p. 49.
24. *Selected Criticism and Prose*, p. 386.
25. *Essays of Introductions*, p. 401.
26. *Selected Criticism and Prose*, p. 387.
27. Denis Donoghue, *Yeats*, p. 51.
28. Yeats, *CP*, p. 223.
29. I have borrowed these views largely from Murray Kricger's *The Classic Vision: The Retreat from Extremity in Modern Literature* in which an elaborate discussion of this idea is found.
30. Yeats, *Autobiographies*, p. 194.
31. *Selected Criticism and Prose*, p. 193.
32. Yeats, *CP*, p. 223.
33. *Ibid.*, p. 333.
34. Yeats, *Autobiographies*, p. 246.
35. Yeats, *CP*, pp. 223-24.
36. J.B. Yeats, *W.B. Yeats: A Critical Anthology*, p. 67.
37. Herbert Read, *The True Voice of Feeling: Studies in English Romantic Poetry* (London: Faber and Faber, 1968), p. 151.
38. Owen Barfield, "The Philosophy of S.T. Coleridge," *Romanticism Comes of Age* (London: Rudolf Steiner Press, 1944), pp. 157-58.
39. Owen Barfield, *What Coleridge Thought* (London: OUP, 1972), p. 158.
40. *Biographia Literaria*, ed. George Watson (1906; rpt. London: Dent, 1977), p. 167.
41. *Ibid.*, pp. 173-74.
42. *Ibid.*, p. 167.
43. M.H. Abrams, *The Mirror and the Lamp: Romantic Theory and the Tradition* (London: OUP, 1960), p. 118.
44. *Selected Criticism and Prose*, p. 187.
45. Raymond Benoit, *Single Nature's Double Name*, p. 5.
46. Cleanth Brooks, "I.A. Richards and the Concept of Tension," in

I.A. Richards: Essays in His Honour, p. 152.

47. Murray Krieger, *The New Apologists for Poetry* (Bioomington: Indiana Univ. Press, 1963), p. 121.
48. *Ibid.*
49. Octavio Paz, *Children of the Mire*, p. 45.
50. Yeats, *CP*, p. 217.
51. Robert Penn Warren, *Selected Essays*, p. 29.
52. Denis Donoghue, *The Sovereign Ghost: Studies in Imagination* (London: Faber and Faber, 1978), p. 18.
53. *Ibid.*, p. 2.
54. Denis Donoghue, *The Ordinary Universe*, p. 133.
55. Yeats, *CP*, p. 7.
56. Denis Donoghue, *The Sovereign Ghost*, p. 6.
57. Yeats, *Autobiographies*, p. 274.
58. Krieger, *The New Apologists*, p. 26.
59. Frank Kermode, p. 19.
60. Octavio Paz, p. 56.
61. Allen Tate, *The Man of Letters in the Modern World: Selected Essays: 1928-55* (1955; New York: Meridian Books, 1964), p. 97.
62. R.P. Blackmur, *The Lion and the Honeycomb* (New York: Harcourt and Brace, 1954), p. 153.
63. Yeats, *Autobiographies*, p. 482.
64. Allen Tate, p. 112.
65. Yeats, *CP*, p. 392.
66. Allen Tate, p. 103.
67. *Ibid.*, p. 112.
68. *Ibid.*
69. Yeats, *CP*, pp. 266-67.
70. *Ibid.*, p. 339.

Making of the Self

In 1888, speaking about his early poetry in one of his letters, Yeats admitted that it was "almost all a flight into faeryland from the real world, and a summons to that flight." It was a poetry "of longing and complaint—the cry of the heart against necessity." But he hoped to overcome this someday, and write a poetry "of insight and knowledge."[1] If "someday setting out to find knowledge, like some pilgrim to the Holy Land," he becomes the "most romantic of characters" and begins to "play with all masks,"[2] it is because the complicated and labyrinthine way to "knowledge and insight" is fraught with hazards, especially when by knowledge we mean "self-knowledge." If Yeats came anywhere near this ideal he had set for himself, his achievement may be attributed, as Eliot put it, to an innate capacity for experience. He found himself in "a different world in every decade of his life." Since he saw it each time with feelings natural to that stage, and "with different eyes, the material of his art is continually renewed."[3]

Yeats explained that for a lyric poet "every kind of subtlety, obscurity, and intricate utterance prevails, for the human spirit has begun to look in upon itself with microscopic eyes and to judge of ideas and feelings apart from their effects upon action. . . . In a lyric age the poets no longer can take their inspiration mainly from external activities and from what are called matters of fact, for they must express every phase of human consciousness no matter how subtle, how vague, how impalpable."[4] With this subtlety, the poetry "steps out of the market-place, out of the general tide of life and becomes a mysterious cult, as it were, an almost secret religion made by the few for the few."[5] The French Symbolists sought to achieve a pure form of poetry which would be close in refinement to music, and in doing so stepped out of the "market-place" and the "general tide of life." As a lyric poet, Yeats also must have felt the temptation to enter into this rarefied world. If he did not yield and instead learnt that when "a man is to write lyric poetry he must be shaped by nature and art to some one out of half a dozen traditional poses, and be lover or saint, sage or sensualist, or mere mocker of all life" and none but that "stroke of luckless luck can open before him the accumulated expression of the world,"[6] it is because he had pledged himself to the human situation and the idea that a poet "should know all classes of men." He wanted to be able to combine "the greatest possible personal realization" with "the greatest possible knowledge of the speech and circumstances of the world."[7]

All this did not come easily. What began as a weak struggle to fulfil private dream in romantic poetry became a dominant conflict of both life and poetry, rendering them into artefacts of immense and vital experience. This does not mean, however, that the conflict which had begun as a flight from the real world underwent no essential change. The body of Yeats's poetry went through a metamorphosis within itself, while organically it remained the same.

The early poetry of Yeats forms the seminal phase which provides a basis for future development. Yeats did not become a new poet at every stage. Learning from past mistakes of the man and artist, he rose to the maturity of a great poet on the stepping stones of his own dead selves. Each phase of his poetic career represents a certain way of looking at things. There is a conscious, well-planned and "deliberate shaping" of poems to make them belong to a particular phase, suggesting that Yeats wanted each volume of his poetry to represent a certain "mood," and the whole body of poetry to stand for the man, a "community of moods." Literature differs from scientific writing in its "being wrought about a mood, or a community of moods, as the body is wrought about an invisible soul."[8] It wants to make us "partakers at the banquet of moods," which are the "labourers and messengers of the Ruler of All, the Gods of ancient days still dwelling on their secret Olympus, the angels of more modern days ascending and descending upon their shining ladder."[9] All "argument, theory, erudition, observation, are merely what Blake called 'little devils who fight for themselves,' illusions of our visible passing life, who must be made to serve the moods."[10] The mysterious instinct of the artist teaches him to discover "moods in mortal desires, an undecaying hope in our trivial ambitions, a divine love in sexual passion."[11]

Each "mood," each way of looking at life, was carefully outlined. The attempt was to consciously shape both art and life. Yeats revised his early poems when he felt the necessity to order them to fit the frame he had in mind. What matter if it be deliberate art? One must "labour to be beautiful." What courtesy and self-possession are to life, style is in art. Both are "the sensible impressions of the free mind, for both arise out of a deliberate shaping of all things, and from never being swept away, whatever the emotions, into confusion or dullness."[12]

For Yeats, the reconstruction of art was as important as the reconstitution of the Self. In its being "reconstituted," the self does not become less "sincere." Yeats did not see any contradiction in this. According to him, the process of identity-making could go on for a number of lives. While the old idea of "sincerity" calls up the "unreconstructed self," the new "sincerity" reveals the "reconstructed self." And if one's life is embodied in one's poems, then perfection of the art would naturally be linked to the perfection of life, and thereby call for a "deliberate shaping" of things.

"A man's life is one thing and then another, a poet's life is his *Collected Poems*,"[13] says Denis Donoghue, and perhaps this is more true in Yeats's case than anybody else's. Yeats had begun with the aim of making his life a work of art. To make this work of art embody the variety and diversity of life, he needed to cultivate several interests—which is why he is often, unfortunately, mistaken for an occultist, politician and rhetorician rather than poet. Though there was the fear at one time that a "woman's face" might tempt him from his craft and he would, on a reckless impulse, throw "poor words" away—he himself confessed:

All things can tempt me from this craft of verse:
One time it was woman's face, or worse—
The seeming needs of my fool-driven land[14]

—none of these interests, whether it was love of a woman, or "theatre-business, management of men," or politics, could ultimately divert him from his first love: Poetry.

Now nothing but comes readier to the hand
Than this accustomed toil.[15]

All the other interests, which were outside the realm of poetry, were assimilated into this central, wholly-absorbing passionate love. Even his "instructors" had come not to teach him doctrinal wisdom but to give him "metaphors for poetry." When the Life is in the Poetry, a poet's chief preoccupation would be with the poetic mode. But, when the Life is the Poetry, nothing remains outside its precincts. Yeats was deeply involved in the poetics of living. He gave everything poetic treatment. Each rude and incongruous form of life ministered to the one rule that it make itself amenable to the poet's formative touch and allow itself to be moulded and fashioned into an artifice of eternity. It is always the art that is important, particularly its formal element. The poem holds supremacy over the experience.

Since poetry is made out of a quarrel with ourselves, conflict is wooed, courted as it were, for its engendering quality. It is cultivated for the energy it generates to propel and commence another conflict. Nor is it intended to end in resolution. Yeats's mind was restless

> with finality, because finality is peace or death. Those who say that Yeats was a Platonist are right, subject to the qualification that he was the opposite, empiricist or realist, even on the same occasion. If we select a value and say it is dear to Yeats, we may be right, but only if we allow equal recognition to its opposite.[16]

The strength in the poetry came from an equal and opposite participant in the quarrel. The conflicting force can operate from the outside, but the quarrel is always greater, more productive and powerful when it is enacted within a single poem and in the same mind. An equal intensity of conflict may be generated in both cases. But, when the quarrel is between two persons, it is a "war to the death." When the battle is waged in the same mind, it is "war to the life," not to the death. This would ensure that at the end of the battle it is life that remains, not death. There is a sense not of defeat or loss, but of achievement, no matter who wins.

In its being internal and located in the same mind, the conflict is typical of all romantic poetry. As the "last romantic" Yeats sought to bridge the gulf between opposing impulses by bringing them as convincingly close as possible. The idea of self-transformation or "reconstituted self" is common to romanticism. Also, the Romantic imagination is "free" in the sense that it can play a number of roles, as in a drama, like Yeats's "half a dozen traditional poses," and shape and modify the self. The poet is both creator and actor, spectator and participant in his own work. The conflict is three-fold—that between the poet and persona, poem and poet, and, a third more commonly acknowledged, between the personae in the poem.

In the early poetry of Yeats, wherein the verse is generally imitative in style, the conflict remained largely vague and peripheral. There is very little attempt at realism, and the poet struggles to lift the burden of the "past" by attempting to emulate early writers, especially Spenser and Shelley. The predominant mood is one of other-worldliness. And, the themes are drawn from Celtic legends and ballads. The verse is dreamy and misty, the manner descriptive but external and weak. *The Cloak, the Boat and the Shoes* has a poignancy about it that keeps us enthralled in its spell of sorrow, while the pensive quality of *Ephemera* captivates by its simple nostalgic tone. In *The Stolen Child* and *To an Isle in the Water*, Yeats is a singer of lyrical song or, at best, a poet dreaming of escape. Though the human child of *The Stolen Child* is lured away from a world "more full of weeping than you can understand," he will miss

> the lowing
> Of the calves on the warm hillside
> Or the kettle on the hob
> Sing peace into his breast,
> Or see the brown mice bob
> Round and round the oatmeal-chest.[17]

—all images of the lively, pulsating world of warm peace and busy growing.

Uneasily balanced between two kingdoms—one, which he has cast away to the "young subtle Conchubar" but whose burden he still feels upon his head, and the other, which the Druid can give him, the "dreaming wisdom" of the ancient mind—Fergus is restless with his "little bag of dreams." Perhaps, it would have been better to have chosen a woman's love or laboured, even if foolishly, to be another's dream. Fergus finds he has "grown nothing, knowing all." And, what has Fergus known? That "great webs of sorrow" lie "hidden in the small slate-coloured thing!"? Everywhere, even in a dreaming wisdom, the poet is greeted by sorrow, by the impossibility of finding a perfect frame to fit in happiness. "Dream" still disappoints him, and, as it dwindles into unreality, prepares Yeats for the gradual acceptance of the breathing life of change he wanted to get away from. The major motif of Yeats's later poetry that an absolute condition is impossible, that every choice between opposites is relative is prefigured in Fergus.

Poems like the long narrative *The Wanderings of Oisin*, and *The Lake Isle of Innisfree* and *The Man Who Dreamed of Faeryland* show his increasing interest in European symbolism. In protesting against the scientific age, the Symbolists sought to find a substitute-world superior to the real world of the senses. It was the contention of the Ideal against Reality. In their search for the Ideal and Beautiful, the pioneers of the Symbolist Movement like Baudelaire in France and Pater in England relied on a rarefied world of art. Pater proclaimed art as a worthy aim of life because it offered a relatively "quickened multiplied consciousness." Unlike the French Symbolist Movement which was mystical, English Aestheticism had a touch of the Impressionist school. In their conviction that their ideal world could be realized in art, the symbolists avoided public and political themes. Though undeniably rich and intense, their world remained narrow and self-centred. Its chief asset and contribution was that it recovered the subjective element in poetry. While the art was regarded as primarily impersonal, the artist expressed, in fact, his own idiosyncratic and remarkable view of the world, and the self became a rich subject for poetry. To bring in the elements of music, symbolist poetry attempted to create a pure, mystic "atmosphere." Since the symbolist poet staunchly believed in the inadequacy of the plain or direct statement, he adopted the artistic mode of suggestion. But, no matter how beautiful the world of the Pure Symbolist, it was cut off from the man in the street. It was elitist in orientation. By concentrating on private vision, the artist estranged himself from a large part of life—the world of strife. By persistently living in a world removed from the common life of the crowd, he created a rift between poetry and ordinary life, and deprived himself of the strength of a poetry that is rooted to the earth. A poetry made of "words," a merely verbal beauty of "sound" rather than "sense," however perfect it may be, is limited in terms of the totality of experience. The successors of the Symbolists, while they accepted the ideas of their predecessors, moved away from an art which was a private, confined and mystical experience to one which reunited itself to public life.

The symbolist influence in Yeats, noticeable in the initial stages of his poetic career, faded away after a time. Unlike the Symbolists, Yeats did not feel deeply the immediate impact of science on peasant culture and private life. He lived in a country where "the tide of life is rising" and "we turn, not to picture-making, but to the imagination of personality—to drama, gesture."[18] In Ireland, "personality" was still as important as it had been in the eighteenth century. The beauty and spontaneity of peasant thought was retained "unspoiled by the artificial town-made thought."[19]

Yeats was aware of the fact that the scientific movement had brought with it "a literature which was always tending to lose itself in externalities of all kinds, in opinion, in declamation, in picturesque writing, in word-painting, or in what Mr. Symons has called an attempt 'to build in brick and mortar inside the covers of a book'."[20] The symbolist influence upon Yeats was marked but was only a temporary and short-lived phase. A few traces of its influence can be seen in *The Wanderings of Oisin* and *The Song of Wandering Aengus*, both narrative poems written in the manner of the Pre-Raphaelites. In these poems Yeats does not seem to make any effort at realism. The aim is rather to give the dramatic suggestion of a painting.

In *The Song of the Happy Shepherd*, the poet begins by saying that the woods of Arcady are dead, and words "alone are certain good." He does not wish to worship "dusty deeds,"

> Nor seek, for this is also sooth,
> To hunger fiercely after truth,
> Lest all thy toiling only breeds
> New dreams, new dreams[21]

because

> there is no truth
> Saving in thine own heart.

Instead it would be better, he says, to "Go gather by the humming sea,"

> Some twisted, echo-harbouring shell,
> And to its lips thy story tell,
> And they thy comforters will be,
> Rewording in melodious guile
> Thy fretful words a little while,
> Till they shall singing fade in ruth
> And die a pearly brotherhood.[22]

Though this advice is given, the poet does not take comfort from the rewording of "fretful words." It is all a "melodious *guile*," giving the false impression of sweet music. The poet knows that dreams are half-truths and deceitful. Dreams escape from harsh reality. But, though he knows that it is all deception, and only "guile," he permits himself to be deceived because he is not yet ready to fit in both worlds—the real and the ideal, the world of his experience ("full of weeping") and the world of dreams ("a faeryland"). He is not yet prepared for the transition from dream to reality.

After *The Song of the Happy Shepherd,* the Sad Shepherd realized that a shell to which he thought he would tell his "heavy story":

> Till my own words, re-echoing, shall send
> Their sadness through a hollow, pearly heart;
> And my own tale again for me shall sing,
> And my own whispering words be comforting,[23]

and his "ancient burden may depart," has only changed what he sang to it into "inarticulate moan," "forgetting him."

Dream and the Beautiful are seen to be unmindful of the sorrow of life. Beauty holds no comfort, so far removed it is from the realities of the world in which the poet lives. As early as *The Song of the Sad Shepherd*—the sad shepherd ends up with having to carry his own ancient burden of sadness—Yeats seemed to vaguely associate the Ideal and the Beautiful with proud unconcern and cold indifference to the sad toil and tale of ordinary man. The ephemerality of the Symbolist mode, for Yeats, may be explained by its inadequacy to adapt itself to the poet's deepest and fullest experience.

In the early Yeats, the search for Unity remained uncertain and indistinct. Unity is "stated," but no attempt is made to "earn" it. There is not the mature realization that real Unity embodies "both—and," all opposites. As yet, Yeats is only a dreamer who wishes to escape to a world of glorious harmony and bliss. If there is any suggestion of a more-than-dreamlike disregard in the rejection of the common world, an attempt, though a feeble one, to achieve Unity, it is to be seen as an almost desperate effort to enfold both worlds in the hope that it would save him from having to discard the more beautiful one of bliss and gaiety. The conflict is based on sharp contrasts, not on equally attractive and powerful elements.

Under the influence of Arthur Symons, Yeats gave up the simple, easy style of the early period, and adopted a "more, elaborate, studied" one in its place. Yeats accepted the view that symbols are essential to poetry. According to him, symbols are of two kinds. Emotional symbols are those where "sound, and colour, and form are in a musical relation, a beautiful relation to one another," and become as it were, "one sound, one colour, one form, and evoke an emotion that is made out of their distinct evocations and yet is one emotion."[24] An Intellectual symbol evokes "ideas alone, or ideas mingled with emotions."[25]

Yeats's method was to take some character from folklore or legend and express through it his own emotional state. The conflict in his mind was externalized in the mythological figure. It is in this sense that the bard in *The Song of Wandering Aengus* becomes a symbol of personal longing for a "glimmering girl/ With apple blossom in her hair"—a vivid recollection of Maud Gonne as she looked on their first meeting.

The warrior Cuchulain's lingering love for a woman he had met in passing during one of his battle-marches through the forests, his deep yearning for a child that she could have borne him, and his moral defeat at the hands of the son she bore him without his knowledge, show that in Cuchulain Yeats saw a strong man of action thoughtful over a woman he could not forget. The wandering hero that Cuchulain is, he still has deep down in him the homing instinct. Perhaps, the poet found in Cuchulain the figure of a man who, bound by action, was drawn to the contemplation of a lovely woman. Early in life, Yeats recognized that the poetic instinct made the meditative mood an aspect of his life. He felt inferior, in some way, to other men devoted to an active existence. To compensate, Yeats wrote of legendary heroes of Ireland that were a direct counterpart of him but who retained, at the same time, enough of the love of the imaginative life for him to be able to partly identify himself with them. As Brenda Webster rightly points out, through legendary heroes of Ireland Yeats increased his "capacity to replay emotional traumas with himself in control, to turn passive suffering into active mastery."[26] But when David Lynch argues against these rather oversimplified psychoanalytic answers, he is, perhaps, justifiably refusing to explain the poet's compulsion to re-create his precursors in terms of a simple "oedipal" argument. Although Bloom might feel that a poet's sense of his precursors and his achievement in relation to theirs constitutes the anxiety of poetic influence, in Yeats's case it was, as Lynch suggests, a deep need to "create" the oedipal *antagonist,* not because of any narcissistic trait, but as "an expression of his even more fundamental need to create himself."[27] In turning from verbal picture-making to the making of a personality, from "words alone" to drama and gesture, Yeats made a major departure. It completely changed the direction his poetry was to take. It affected his attitude to poetry-making, relative to the idea of sincerity and reality, the persona and the person.

Yeats's symbolism always tended to be more emotional than intellectual. The Rose of his poems is a symbol not only of love and perfect beauty, but also of Ireland, the spiritual country to which he was emotionally attached. Again, it is an idealized country, not the political Ireland of his day. The Rose is also related to the wor of his dreams.

We see, in *To the Rose Upon the Rood of Time,* the poet aware of the inherent conflict in his love for the Ideal country of Ireland and the real Ireland in which he lived. This underlying conflict is reflected in his address to the "Red Rose, proud Rose, sad Rose of all my days!":

> Come near me while I sing the ancient ways.

But even as he says this, the poet is afraid,

Lest I no more hear common things that crave;
The weak worm hiding down in its small cave,
The field-mouse running by me in the grass,
And heavy mortal hopes that toil and pass;

and, enamoured of eternal beauty,

But seek alone to hear the strange things said
By God to the bright hearts of those long dead,
And learn to chaunt a tongue men do not know.[28]

If he learns to "chaunt a tongue men do not know," he will lose the common touch, the "emotion of multitude," and belie the poetic ideal he had set before him of reaching to "upstanding men" that are "Bound neither to Cause nor to State," the people of Burke and of Grattan. Therefore, he appeals to the Rose to come near, but not too near—"Ah, leave me still," he says,

A little space for the rose-breath to fill!

The poet who wrote in the short lyric *The Lake Isle of Innisfree:*

I will arise and go now, for always night and day
I hear lake water lapping with low sounds by the shore;
While I stand on the roadway, or on the pavements grey,
I hear it in the deep heart's core[29]

was a romanticist who, Icarus-like, wanted to free himself from the complexities of life and fly to a dream-world where "peace comes dropping slow." After such flight to Ideal land to have to return to the Real world must have meant great effort. It would not have been easy for the poet of *The Lake Isle of Innisfree* to say later in *The Coming of Wisdom with Time:*

Though leaves are many, the root is one;

Through all the lying days of my youth
I swayed my leaves and flowers in the sun;
Now I may wither into the truth.[30]

He could not, in other words, have said it without its having been authenticated by an inner change of outlook. There was a craving to escape to an Isle of Peace and Joy, a beautiful fictional world of no sorrow. There was also a reluctance to shake off or reject the ordinary world. Between both these opposing impulses, the course he finally took—a return to the Real—establishes, beyond doubt, the fact that the poet took this decision after a profound consideration of the relative value of life.

His veering away from Symbolism to the oral tradition of Ireland may be explained by an insistence to place Man at the centre or, alternately, to make the centre Man. His Muse was trying to discover a self that would uphold and support the whole body and meaning of his poetry. If Yeats's

> characteristic poems are cries, laments, prayers, stories, legends, rebukes; human sounds[31]

it is not because he neglected "to 'make' his poems. It means that the making of a poem, for him, largely consisted in making the sounds more and more responsive to a human occasion, real or imagined."[32]

Yeats's early work couched the inner struggle under a symbolic guise. The timid self, faced with "the ignominy of growing up" and the "distress of boyhood changing into man," chose, in its search for selfhood, to identify itself with its counterparts in Irish legendary heroes. The conflict which was shrouded in vague and "poetical" terms, is finally thwarted when the poet finds the ideal vain and elusive—Oisin returns from the Isle of Forgetfulness to confront a new world championed by St. Patrick, Cuchulain's fight with the sea becomes a struggle with the invulnerable tide, Aedh as the defeatist lover sings of love but with sadness, and the Man who dreamed of Faeryland has found "no comfort in the grave." The conflict presented through characters which are, as Wright says, "in the best romantic tradition, poetic exaggerations of the aspirations of the poet: Oisin, Aengus, Forgael,"[33] undergoes a conversion from "poetic" to "dramatic" when it no longer remains the simple one between a painful and dark world and a world of beauty and perfect gaiety, but becomes the more difficult one between two equally desirable things. It is here that Unity achieved in terms of a reconciliation of opposites comes in. As one who took both life and art seriously, Yeats was never tired of showing how many were the ways in which the unity finally achieved was duly earned. If Unity is enacted dramatically in terms of a dialectical tension, it could prevent its being mistaken for a simple and superficial one. So a dialectical tension between two entities equally desirable is what becomes characteristic of Yeats's later poetry.

The transition from the early, to the later style was achieved in terms of a gradual change from vagueness and generalization to a hardness and definite strength that comes out of personal utterance. "Personal utterance," or "the actual thoughts of a man at a passionate moment of life," which had "almost ceased in English literature, could be as fine an escape from rhetoric and abstraction as drama itself."[34]

Yeats's poetry, then, may be said to be built upon a system of contraries, on an arrangement of values in antithesis. In becoming aware of both good and bad, harmony and anarchy, action and contemplation, Yeats's approach becomes not only more realistic but that much more poignant. In *Down by the Salley Gardens,* the lady tells her lover to "take love easy,"

> But I, being young and foolish, with her would not agree.

The lady is as wise as she is fair. She bids him "take life easy," but he is so enchanted by her "snow-white" beauty that he does not need her warning. He had thought his dream-love would last, and now is "full of tears."[35] There is an indefinable sadness about this poem and the later one, *After Long Silence.* The ignorance, foolishness and immaturity of youth which takes the romantic dream very seriously is shown to suffer the pain of truth in old age. Both poems seem to recognize the pathos of wrong choices and, yet, both see pain as an inevitable fact of existence. Truth hits harder the man who is deceived. The less deceived would be hurt less. But, in younger days one is deceived by the Dream. As the lovers descant, "curtains drawn upon unfriendly night," on the "supreme theme of Art and Song," there comes the recognition that pain is, perhaps, a value. As in *Down by the Salley Gardens*, *After Long Silence* associates youth with ignorance and romantic love. With maturity comes realization, the awareness that wisdom follows "bodily decrepitude" and one withers, as it were, into truth when one does not have the strength any more to act on that wisdom.

Though by the time *The Wind Among the Reeds* and *In the Seven Woods* came out, Yeats had given up much of the early aestheticism and was trying to become a man of action, the poetry still reveals a faint, lingering influence of the French Symbolists. If their symbolism differed from what Yeats practised, it was because they made poetry a magical incantation without meaning, whereas, though Yeats performed a kind of verbal magic, he knew the proper place of "rhetoric," and was sensitive to the dramatic word and sound. Moreover, he was uncompromisingly committed to write a poetry that would remain firmly rooted to the basic concerns of life. By placing an exaggerated value on emotion rather than intellect, the French Symbolists estranged the poet from the everyday world. "As for living, our servants will do that for us," they said. Under their influence, Yeats wrote poems like *He Wishes for the Cloths of Heaven*, *The Cap and Bells*, etc. The influence of the French Symbolists brought about a deepening of his poetry since without imitating them, he tried to perform the miracle they were performing.

The Green Helmet and Other Poems shows in Yeats the awakening of a new poetic consciousness. A political interest which had been absent before enters his poetry. The real, everyday world is posited alongside the ideal. In learning to come to terms with life, Yeats was slowly moving toward that Unity of Being which, in his later life, he interpreted as that deep peace which overpowers man when in tragic gaiety he converts practical defeat into aesthetic triumph. In earlier poems like *To the Rose Upon the Rood of Time, To Ireland in the Coming Times, The Secret Rose, Red Hanrahan's Song About Ireland,* he addresses the Rose as an Ideal Ireland of Everlasting beauty, asking her to reveal herself to him. This is not the political Ireland of his times. Yeats's Ireland of the *Rose* poems is a fiction, the idealized Ireland of undying innocence, a symbol of pride and faith, beauty and power. It is hardly possible that when he invokes her as:

> Red Rose, proud Rose, sad Rose of all my days![36]
>
> Rose of all Roses, Rose of all the World![37]
>
> Far-off, most secret, and inviolate Rose[38]

or calls her "Cathleen, the daughter of Houlihan"[39] Yeats has in mind the real Ireland, fraught with political strife. It is only in this volume that any indication is given to us of a realistic approach to the affairs of the country. The burning faith is still there but it is partly replaced by an acridity which has come from having to face the reality of things, earlier merely hinted at in *Red Hanrahan's Song* by the use of phrases like "bitter black wind," "noisy clouds," "heavy flooded waters." In Hanrahan's Song, the devotion to the purity of Ireland persisted. Nothing could harm, he thought, this symbol of valour, though an atmosphere of threat surrounded her. He says:

> Our courage breaks like an old tree in a black wind and dies,
> But we have hidden in our hearts the flame out of the eyes
> Of Cathleen, the daughter of Houlihan.[40]

Cathleen is associated with Virgin Mary and the Cross, and, therefore, what is offered to her is almost a religious worship. The Symbolist influence has still not completely faded away but, with an entry into the period of *The Green Helmet and Other Poems,* we find the poet more responsible and realistic. His love for Maud Gonne has been frustrated by her revolutionary zeal, and the painful experience of having lost her to Ireland can be seen in a poem like *No Second Troy*. Maud Gonne, the "Helen" and "Phoenix" of his poems, was a poetic symbol of Ireland. She symbolized, for the poet, superior power wasted on a worthless, unequal cause in the absence of one more worthy and noble. The poet finds that he has grown old loving her. There is also the greater unhappiness that she has sacrificed herself for something inferior, and for a people who are too vulgar to appreciate the sacrifice. Even if we do not read this poem as autobiography, we are aware that the woman the speaker loved is a modern version of Helen who, in the absence of another Troy to burn, "would have taught to ignorant men most violent ways" had they but "courage equal to desire." "Why should I blame her," he says, "that she filled my days/ With misery?"[41] What could have made her peaceful with a mind and beauty unnatural in an age like ours? She had to find some way of venting herself out. As an attempt to justify her revolutionary zeal, even when it operated against the fulfilment of his love's desire, this poem is a poignant expression of the supreme endurance of love. Though his love for Maud Gonne has been fruitless, loving her has made him a poet. The man's loss has been the poet's gain. Perhaps if she had reciprocated the love, he "might have thrown poor words away/ And been content to live." He cannot deny, however, that Maud by becoming a revolutionary has done harm not only to herself but also to others by preaching violence. And *No Second Troy*, where he offers a kind of apology for her despite the fact that he hated violence, is a moving tribute to her—a fine gesture on the part of the poet. He is able to see opposites in combination—virtue and vice in a kind of balance. There is the realization that life is organized only in terms of thesis and antithesis. With her kind of mind "that nobleness made simple as a fire," and with beauty "like a tightened bow":

> Being high, and solitary and most stern?
> Why, what could she have done, being what she is?

Was there another Troy for her to burn?[42]

In equating her with Helen of Troy, he has not only offered a homage to her beauty, but also acknowledged its perils. *No Second Troy* anticipates *Leda and the Swan* where the speaker asks:

So mastered by the brute blood of the air,
Did she put on his knowledge with his power
Before the indifferent beak could let her drop?[43]

When such beauty is dissociated from its direct opposite—knowledge—it cannot but have dangerous consequences for the individual and the people in the midst of whom such beauty is born.

The experiences that preceded *Responsibilities* brought Yeats in open confrontation with the "fumbling wits" of his country. Yeats has begun to face reality. Having been a witness to a dispute between a nobleman who offered to give pictures to the Dublin Municipality if a picture gallery was built, and a wealthy man who promised a second subscription to the construction of the building if it was proved that the people wanted the pictures, and having seen the open vulgarity and commercial attitudes of the blind and ignorant town, Yeats scorns the men of his time for having belied the romantic traditions of the Ireland of Old.

His disillusionment with the common people, who proved unworthy of leaders like O'Leary, Pearse, Edward Fitzgerald and others, made him write *September 1913* wherein he angrily says:

What need you, being come to sense,
But fumble in a greasy till
And add the halfpence to the pence
And prayer to shivering prayer, until
You have dried the marrow from the bone?
For men were born to pray and save:
Romantic Ireland's dead and gone,
It's with O'Leary in the grave.[44]

Yeats's interest in politics was restricted to "a powerful relation to 'the people'." What he admired in Hyde, Davis or Parnell was not so much the poetry as their ability to "speak out of a people to a people." He respected Lady Gregory because she was interested in Irish folklore, the "book of the people." He was not interested in revolutionary and radical politics. It is a mistake to think he coveted political power. He wanted power, of course, but it was moral power he wanted, not political power. And he wanted it to order his life. If he appeared rhetorical, it was because in the Ireland to which he belonged "the governing art is rhetoric, proof of power is voice." This is the reason why he sought, "not as Wordsworth thought, words in common use, but a powerful and passionate syntax."[45] "All must be an idealization of speech, and at some moment of passionate action or somnambulistic reverie."[46] All must be a "discussion of style." In an oral culture, like Ireland's, experience is passed on through speech and lore. It is a "continuity of voice from generation to generation."[47] For Yeats, tradition was voice or "emotion of multitude."

The transitional period in Yeats's poetry, between the early and later phase, is marked by a gradual renunciation of the misty and dream-like quality of much of the earlier verse, and a lesser reliance on elaborate mythology and folklore, a turning away from "islands" and a return to "earth." In *A Coat,* with which the *Responsibilities* volume ends, Yeats makes a formal announcement of the new direction that his poetry is to take. He relinquishes "old mythologies," in preference for the greater enterprise of "walking naked." The "embroideries" are set aside because they have become redundant to the theory of the mask that he developed in *Per Amica*--that a poet while engaged in the creative act is actually seeking not his self, but a mask which is his anti-self. He wrote in 1909:

> I think that all happiness depends on the energy to assume the mask of some other life, on a rebirth as something not one's self.[48]

In adherence to this aesthetic theory, he invented his own mythical system or "private mythology" of fictitious selves to act as dramatic metaphors for a more powerful mode of expression. By putting on masks he could gain creative power and also discover himself. In his belief that a self can complete itself only by assuming a mask of its direct opposite, the anti-self, Yeats was close to Jung's idea of individuation. Lillian Feder writes in her book *Ancient Myth in Modern Poetry:*

> like Jung, he seeks the immortal in the human psyche.[49]

What Yeats wanted was to express a general truth out of intense personal experience. In this kind of impersonality, the poet retains all the particularity of his experience and yet makes of it a general symbol. Beneath the masks, there is still a deep desire to be truly one's self. The masks helped Yeats to assume various "voices" without losing the intensity of specific experience. The masks gave him both "a lone individual voice" as well as universal relevance. As Michael Schmidt says:

> The mythological autobiography is powerful because the 'I-myth' replaces the baseless 'we-myth' of the earlier poems. Yeats begins to stress the unique individual experience.[50]

The problem was how one could speak in a personal voice in order not to lose one's particular identity among myriad voices, and also speak for all men to give poetry an enduring universal meaning. Ellmann puts it lucidly when he writes that though Yeats ostensibly gave up his old coat, embroidered with mythologies, in preference for the greater enterprise of walking naked, "nakedness has itself become an artifice for him. His search now will be for a variety of dramatic situation in which to pretend to be naked."[51] The search for a "dramatic metaphor" is directly linked to the quest for Unity because in it the poet can enact conflict, making the end-unity more credible. Functionally speaking, the dramatic metaphor acts as an ironic mode to fortify the poet's integrity. If after a long and extensive effort to become an impersonal character, a poet does not succeed in concealing himself, and preventing the personal voice from intruding, it is not altogether surprising. Perhaps the only difference between one poet and another who professes a theory of impersonality is how effectively or how poorly one couches the self beneath it all.

The middle period of Yeats's poetry gathers a harder quality as he begins to apply his theory of the mask to it. With the wheel turning round, Yeats is no longer ashamed of conflict. In fact, through the insight and strength of experience gained, he has learned to come to terms with the problems he had evaded in his younger days. In *The Wild Swans at Coole* volume which begins with a poem by the same title, Yeats has become old. He has also undergone the chastening and liberating experience of pain. Beside him and his increasing age, the swans appear still young:

> Their hearts have not grown old;
> Passion or conquest, wander where they will,
> Attend upon them still.[52]

The birds typify permanence in a world of flux. The swans will fly to some other place, re-enact timelessness in another world. Theirs is not a futile love. They do not run after passion. Passion or conquest attends upon them. Mysterious and beautiful, they will continue to fascinate man's eyes and mind.

From *The Wild Swans at Coole* onwards, Yeats's preoccupation with old age continued into his riper years, right up to the end of his life. The experiences natural to youth got delayed in his case since he got married very late in life, and for an intense sensibility like his it would have made a lot of difference. He would have felt the irony of beginning life when the body already started showing signs of old age. Yeats was bitter about this. Perhaps it was more of a boon than he realized it himself. He thrust himself on with a frenzied rage, and continued to write some of his best poetry till his death. Very few poets would have shown such a prolific and rich achievement. As Alvarez put it:

> In Yeats's poetry there is a continual tension between the bitterness of what he says and the strength and sweep with which he says it. Eliot has called him a poet of middle age. He seems to me to be the poet of old age in everything except his creative power. That went on growing.[53]

This idea finds further confirmation in Yeats who said that as he himself grew older his muse grew younger. Quoting these words, MacNeice calls Yeats's poetic development "a study in rejuvenation."[54]

The secret of Yeats's creative prolificacy as also its rich quality lies perhaps in his ability, as Eliot suggests, to experience the emotions appropriate to every stage in life, including old age, with the same intensity as the emotions of youth. The refusal to compromise prolonged his poetic life and also gave it strength, by a corresponding refusal to resolve conflict in favour of any one issue.

Besides old age, one of the most persistent and productive conflicts was that of making a choice between a life of action and one of contemplation. The difficulty was in his not wishing to choose either. Yeats knew that the artist, the man of contemplative mind, is one who must live in isolation if he is to find his victory in image-making. The reward of isolation is the Image. But, ironically, its success results in alienation in a hostile society. The "Image" is at once a boon and a bane. Without it there can be no "victory" for the poet, and with it he remains forever alienated. Frank Kermode makes an intriguing thesis on the "Artist in Isolation" in his exciting book *Romantic Image*. The artist, he says, is "exempt from the normal human orientation towards action and so enabled to intuit those images which are truth, in defiance of the triumphant claims of merely intellectual disciplines."[55] Arnold knew all about the Image and what it cost. Since he was not prepared to pay its price, he abandoned it in exchange for humanitarian pursuits. The difference with Yeats was that though he was equally aware of the problem—he also might have chosen the "management of men"—unlike Arnold, "he did not walk out of his dream, but simply extended it to include everything, and went on being a poet till he died."[56]

If the modern artist suffers from a greater sense of isolation, it is because he finds it more difficult to enact the "daily victory" while he is perpetually divided against himself. Though like the scholar-gipsy he waits for the spark from heaven to fall, his is a weak resolve. Nor is it easy for him to find solitude in the "city" which has become the centre of modern life. Nevertheless, the pain of isolation can be momentarily terminated by the "image." It is in an intense and full moment, a "peak" moment as it is sometimes called, that the "image" is made possible. What Yeats celebrated in Major Robert Gregory was "our perfect man," one who lived a short but rich life which was eventually consumed in a "flare."

In Memory of Major Robert Gregory and *An Irish Airman Foresees His Death* have to be read together because both of them were written to commemorate the same event—the death of Lady Gregory's son, Robert Gregory. In the Major Gregory poem, Gregory is made the symbol of a person in whom contraries are reconciled. He is for Yeats "our Sidney and our perfect man." In him, the courage of a man of action and the sense for colour and line that one finds in a great artist are combined:

> Soldier, scholar, horseman, he
> As 'twere all life's epitome.[57]

The Irish Airman knows that he will meet his fate somewhere among the clouds above. The impulse that drives him is neither ethical nor patriotic. It does not even arise from love of his people. He confesses:

> Those that I fight I do not hate,
> Those that I guard I do not love;
> My country is Kiltartan Cross,
> My countrymen Kiltartan's poor,
> No likely end could bring them loss
> Or leave them happier than before.

Nor law, nor duty bade me fight,
Nor public men, nor cheering crowds,
A lonely impulse of delight
Drove to this tumult in the clouds.[58]

"A lonely impulse of delight," an impulse to resolve the tension between action and contemplation, between "the growing absorption of the dream" and "the desire for society," spurs him on to find his fate among the clouds. For a moment, as he balances the past and the present in his mind, he finds everything else appearing small and worthless, a waste of breath beside "this life, this death." As for the poet, so for the airman, the tension is resolved in a moment of extraordinary fullness but at the cost of life. In this rapturous moment of unique and overwhelming intensity, which is at once life and death, the poem itself becomes an image of a temporary victory over confusion and conflict where dream and action are united. The Unity achieved is full and complete, but its price is higher than what the poet is willing to pay. The airman paid for it with his death. A poet cannot afford such a costly "unity." He will rest content with one which, though full in itself, is only temporarily sustained. The poet will enact it again in another "image."

Denis Donoghue in *The Ordinary Universe* explains that Yeats's idiom was the "acknowledgement of conflict within the single state of man, and at the same time the further acknowledgement that value resides in the conflict itself."[59] If the antithetical elements are not resolved, and a dialectical tension is maintained in the poems, it is not because, as Alex Zwerdling argues, Yeats was trying to avoid the necessity of making a choice. This may be true of the early poetry. But in the later, it is not so much the avoidance of the necessity of choice, as the complexity of making one that Yeats demonstrated. In the process, his philosophy becomes one of contraries and antinomies. The metaphysical tension in the human psyche is made vocal in alternation in a single poem, and, as Andrew Parkin says, a new poem is made wherein he dramatizes "his attitudes by means of conflict, dialogue or confrontation with either the dead, or contemporaries or invented personae, evoked as if by magus or medium to take their places with mythic stature in a shadow-play of ideas."[60]

In *Ego Dominus Tuus,* a dialogue between two invented characters of his phantasmagoria takes place within the "single state of man"—between Hic (what the poet *is)* and Ille (what he *becomes),* his direct opposite. Both Hic and Ille, "caught between the pull of the dark moon and the full," seek self-knowledge—Ille, with the help of an image; and Hic, by finding "myself and not an image." Ille mocks Hic's ambitious aim:

> That is our modern hope, and by its light
> We have lit upon the gentle, sensitive mind
> And lost the old nonchalance of the hand;
> Whether we have chosen chisel, pen or brush,
> We are but critics, or but half create,
> Timid, entangled, empty and abashed,
> Lacking the countenance of our friends.[61]

For Hic, style is found by "sedentary toil" and by "the imitation of great masters." Ille, on the other hand, prefers to "walk in the moon," and because he seeks "an image, not a book," he would "call to the mysterious one" who, as he says:

> Shall walk the wet sands by the edge of the stream
> And look most like me, being indeed my double,
> And prove of all imaginable things
> The most unlike, being my anti-self.[62]

Ille recognizes that the wisdom he seeks can come to him only through a mask that provides a suitable image by which the unconscious, the dark self or the anti-self may speak. And, for this, he has the example of Dante Alighieri and Keats, both of whom sought fulfilment through the expression in art of what they in their life could never obtain. It was a "hunger for the apple on the bough/ Most out of reach?"[63] Yeats knew that without complementarity no balance is possible. He resorted to dialogue as an artistic tool for engendering conflict. Dialogue would give rise to a dramatic conflict which, in turn, would generate another series of conflicts. Through dialogue, the ethics of balance and control is achieved. The Dialogue between Hic and Ille is left unresolved, to be continued once again in another dramatic struggle.

As we enter into the later phase of Yeats's poetry, we find sometimes the tension well-maintained, at other times the balance seeming to tilt either on the side of the self, the heart, nature and imagination, or on the side of the anti-self, the soul, art and the intellect. The poet continues to try to attain to the condition of the daimon, his direct opposite, but often finds it difficult of achievement. The conflict continues unabated without any resolution.

In *The Double Vision of Michael Robartes,*[64] Michael Robartes, a fictional figure from Yeats's mythical system, has a vision in which he sees three people—a Sphinx, a Buddha and a Dancer. They are all seen by the moon's light at its fifteenth night. It is one of those phases of the moon when the mind trembles into stillness and is lost in the contemplation of itself. The Sphinx, part-human, part-animal, gazes upon all things known and unknown "In triumph of intellect/ With motionless head erect." The vision of the Buddha, being fixed "on all things loved, all things unloved," is juxtaposed against the triumph of intellect of the Sphinx. Between these two people is one whose "mind moved yet seemed to stop/ As 'twere a spinning top." "She had outdanced thought" and "Body perfection brought." She is another version of the dancer of *Among School Children,* and her labour is "blossoming or dancing where/ The body is not bruised to pleasure soul." By contemplation, these three have worked the moment to a height where time is overthrown. In an exceptional moment of perfect harmony, the dancer has brought movement and stillness, body and mind into equilibrium. It is the kind of unity Yeats sought but knew to be difficult to attain. Therefore, even in its being momentarily held, it is valuable to the poet. Time and eternity meet in the dancer as in the mind of a man of contemplation.

In *Sailing to Byzantium* which inaugurates *The Tower* volume, Yeats begins by acknowledging the fact of his having grown old when he says:

> That is no country for old men. [65]

There is bitterness, certainly, because the speaker who is a man standing between two worlds—one, where all are caught in a sensual music, and the other, where the soul must "clap its hands and sing, and louder sing"—finds the former "no country for old men." Therefore, he has sailed the seas and come to the holy city of Byzantium, a country for old men, where spiritual life and art merge into one. The last line of the first stanza:

> Caught in that sensual music all neglect
> Monuments of unaging intellect

is ironical, and the irony becomes more powerful when the holy city is moved into the foreground, set against the backdrop of a crowded imagery dealing with life, sensual pleasure and generation. The poet begins by saying that "That is no country for old men" and then goes on to describe that very country with a vividness of detail and concreteness of imagery that is overpowering in its impact. In comparison, Byzantium itself pales into insignificance. In terms of poetic excellence this is perhaps the finest stanza of the poem in which Yeats recreates the life of the instinct. If the speaker has resolved to give up "sensual music," it appears to be a weak resolve. The plea to the sages: "Consume my heart away; sick with desire" has an urgency about it that compulsively looks forward to the song of life the golden bird will ultimately sing. Throughout the poem, contraries are posited against each other— "dying" with "generation," "whatever is begotten, born, and dies" with "monuments of unaging intellect," "sensual music" with the soul's song, "dying animal" ("dying" with "animal") with "artifice of eternity," "golden" with "bough," etc. The Byzantium of the poem is an idealized and symbolic city of the artist. Here the speaker, bringing a heart "sick with desire" but "fastened to a dying animal" comes, hoping to be gathered into an "artifice of eternity" once the "sages standing in God's holy fire" become the singing-masters of his soul. Ironically, though he has made up his mind, "once out of nature," never to take his bodily form from any natural thing, the bird that is set upon the golden bough sings to the lords and ladies of Byzantium only of "what is past, or passing, or to come." The paradox of the bird whose bodily form is made "of hammered gold and gold enamelling" and yet whose song is of life in all its changing forms, is parallel to the dilemma faced by the artist. He cannot write poetry without living "out of nature" in isolation, and yet his song must be about life. He cannot help looking back nostalgically to what life is left behind—without it he is no poet—because it is the source of his inspiration, the spring from which his muse must constantly draw out sustenance for his finest work. Like the golden bird, the artist is also a special kind of person. In being a bird unlike others, because it is golden though it is lifeless, it is superior to the "birds in the trees " to the extent that it represents eternity or permanence. Otherwise, it is only an artifice, nothing real or alive. Similarly, to the extent that he speaks for all people, the artist's is an eternal voice. He represents an eternal order that mythically returns to complete the cycle, though in the process he is sacrificed. Perhaps what troubled Yeats was the poor returns that the artist got from the world which needs him as a scapegoat or Christ-figure in order to obtain redemption from sin. Yeats's problem was whether to live as Catullus or to die an Empodoclean death. He did not wish to choose either. He had to score a point against the gradual loss of the creative instinct with the coming of old age. He wanted to force a victory out of defeat and death, as the Irish airman had done, but without ceasing to be. Though removed from the world of man, the poet must, in order to survive as poet, speak about human life. The golden bird, in its turn, also has to find meaning for itself only in terms of a song whose theme is life. What other theme can its song possibly have? Moore, when he attacked the poem, calling it a contradiction in terms, seems to have missed this deep and sad paradox that lives at the heart of the artist's life.

In the title poem *The Tower*, the poet, faced with the absurdity of "decrepit age" that has been tied to him as "to a dog's tail," finds himself a helpless victim of time. The disillusionment is greater because as he reminisces younger days, he sees that his imagination had not been, even in boyhood, in fact, never was as "excited, passionate, fantastical" as it is now. Nor did he have in boyhood "an ear and eye/ That more expected the impossible." But it seems that he must bid the Muse go pack and

> Choose Plato and Plotinus for a friend
> Until imagination, ear and eye,
> Can be content with argument and deal
> In abstract things; or be derided by
> A sort of battered kettle at the heel.[66]

He seeks an answer by calling up images and memories of the past, and asking a question of them all—Mrs. French, the peasant girl whose beauty commended by a blind poet drove certain men mad and, especially, his antithetical self, Hanrahan—if they also did "Whether in public or in secret rage/ As I do now against old age?" "Does the imagination dwell the most," he asks,

> Upon a woman won or a woman lost?
> If on the lost, admit you turned aside
> From a great labyrinth out of pride,
> Cowardice, some silly over-subtle thought
> Or anything called conscience once.[67]

His swan-song, filled with bitter disappointment, is sung "upon a fading gleam." But "Death shall have no dominion," and so, in a mood of vehement protest, he declares his faith:

> I mock Plotinus' thought
> And cry in Plato's teeth,
> Death and life were not
> Till man made up the whole,
> Made lock, stock and barrel

Out of his bitter soul.[68]

Since man has made death, being dead, we may rise again to dream and so create out of a "poet's imagining and memories of love" another world:

All those things whereof
Man makes a superhuman
Mirror-resembling dream.[69]

Coming from among the "deepening shades" and the "testy delirium" accompanying "dull decrepitude," Yeats's valiant voice, placing man at the axis, because "sun and moon and star, all" would not exist were it not for him, towers over the compelling laws of life—old age, decay and death. Old age brings with it the apprehension that perhaps all has been in vain. The "image" that could have brought a rage

To end all things, to end
What my laborious life imagined, even
The half-imagined, the half-written page;

is lost in a "desolate heaven," and we, finally,

Learn that we were crack-pated when we dreamed.[70]

All talk of honour and truth has turned to naught. "Come let us mock," he says, the great, the wise and the good. The irony is soon turned upon himself:

Mock mockers after that
That would not lift a hand maybe
To help good, wise or great
To bar that foul storm out, for we
Traffic in mockery.[71]

Since unity, as Yeats saw it, combined physical life with spiritual experience, it differed from the kind of integration that Hindu ethics speaks of, wherein a man in quest of his "swadharma" or identity proceeds from one "ashrama" (or "resting place") to another till he comes to the last stage of his life which is spent in contemplation and spiritual search. Such a natural progression does not obtain in poetry or art. It was this kind of pattern that presented a dilemma to Yeats. Integration achieved by sacrificing a part of experience did not satisfy him. He wished to go to heaven but carrying, as Hough puts it, all his sensual baggage with him. So his kind of poetic integration was willing to renounce only the superficial layer, or 'husk' as it were, of the previous stage, while drawing its essence on to the next stage and then integrating it. Such a unity of being is possible only at rare moments in history—a unique moment of moments when the poet may intuitively arrive at, or hit upon, a suitable image that would unify all parts into a single whole. Yeats, like Eliot, saw life as incomplete, but while Eliot put his faith in spiritual perfection, Yeats, with Michaelangelo, stood for the "profane perfection of mankind." In his kind of perfection, the physical and the spiritual had to be necessarily integrated. Out of labour that is as spontaneous as dancing, and, therefore, a "blossoming," Yeats, in the poem *Among School Children*, arrives at the image of the tree and the dancer which embody the nature of the unity he has been striving for.

In the first stanza of *Among School Children,* the speaker, a "sixty-year old smiling public man" and an inspector of schools, walks through the school-room where

> The children learn to cipher and to sing
> To study reading-books and histories,
> To cut and sew, be neat in everything
> In the best modern way.[72]

As the poet views the scene, he is reminded of his own childhood and of a woman he had loved. He wonders what she would have looked like at that age. He dreams of the day when over a "sinking fire" she had narrated to him a tale of a "harsh reproof" that had turned "some childish day to tragedy." And as she told,

> . . . it seemed that our natures blent
> Into a sphere from youthful sympathy,
> Or else, to alter Plato's parable,
> Into the yolk and the white of the one shell.[73]

Now both of them have grown old, beauty become "hollow of cheek," a "mess of shadows." The motif of unity in the second stanza, of "two natures blent into a sphere from youthful sympathy," is blurred in memory with the intrusion of the thought of whether a youthful mother would think her son "with sixty or more winters on his head/ A compensation for the pang of his birth." Though the poet would like to show that "There is a comfortable kind of old scarecrow," he feels uncomfortable before the children when he compares their youth with his own aging body. The images that "animate a mother's reveries" or those that nuns worship, both break hearts. The eternal Presences, object of passion, piety or affection, are "self-born mockers of man's enterprise." Plato, Aristotle and Pythagoras, for all their wisdom, became like all other men "Old clothes upon old sticks to scare a bird." The child, lover and sixty-year-old public man are the changing faces of the same self. Lovers, Mothers or devoted worshippers all suffer and become broken-hearted. The final note is of balanced reconciliation. The antinomies converge in the tree and dancer, and are resolved. Their labour is a blossoming or dancing where

> The body is not bruised to pleasure soul,
> Nor beauty born out of its own despair,
> Nor blear-eyed wisdom out of midnight oil.

In all oral cultures, poetry and dance, which are born out of the mimetic rite, are speech and gesture raised to a magical intensity. While the dancer combines both movement (or gesture) and stillness, poetry is sound carved out of silence. Poetry has to do with words, as the dancer with the body. But, the poet uses words, as the dancer does the "vehicle" of form, to transcend "mere word," while the dancer rises to the transpersonal and transphysical plane, invoking essential meanings—both trying to achieve unity by climbing the ladder of form and meaning against a balance of opposites. This kind of unity can come only after great exercise and patient waiting. The poet has to realize wordless experience in the dramatic power of the "word," as the dancer has to realize the spiritual in the flexibility of the "body" before she can give it loveliness in aesthetic "gesture." In Yeats's poetry, the dancer becomes the symbol of a perfect unity achieved by the assimilation of opposites in the unity of form. Like passion and voice in the poet, rhythm and gesture in the dancer make up the formative principle of unity. Courtesy and ceremony are stylizations of life.

Like Caesar, whose eyes are fixed upon nothing, Maud Gonne, whose feet practise a tinker shuffle, and Michaelangelo, who "with no more sound than the mice can make"[75] moves his hand to and fro, the Sphinx, the Buddha and the dancer of Michael Robartes's Double Vision achieve in contemplation a perfection whereby the "mind moved yet seemed to stop/ As 'twere a spinning top"[76] their minds like a "long-legged fly upon the stream" move upon silence.

The dancer of *Among School Children,* combining movement and stillness, dissolves in her dance the distinctions between herself, the music and the dance. By outdancing thought, she has "body perfection brought." And, as for the chestnut tree, one is apt of ask the great-rooted blossomer:

> Are you the leaf, the blossom or the bole?

It is not enough, however, to find the image. One must be able to sustain it. Zwerdling is of the opinion that though "visionary experience is within man's scope, the ultimate fruition is still denied to the Yeatsian seer: his 'vision' does not last."[77] However, it is difficult to believe that the momentariness of visionary experience is the exclusive lot of the Yeatsian seer. Can a unified vision be sustained at all? In Yeats's *Solomon and the Witch,* this problem is pre-figured at the level of physical union when the crow which crowed in eternity from a blossoming apple-bough three hundred years before the Fall, in the union of Solomon and Sheba,

> Chance being at one with Choice at last. . .
> Thought to have crowed it in again,

because "the world ends when these two things,/ Though several, are a single light."[78] The cock crows, but the world stays. While choice and chance have been united temporarily, deluding the cock which thought it "worth a crow," the union does not last. In the cry of Sheba:

> O! Solomon! let us try again

the poet has voiced the anguish of the tragic futility of man's attempt to permanently unite two opposites. Unity may be possible at the purely spiritual level or the level of essence. But Yeats did not want to have anything to do with a poetry made of essences. He had already pledged himself to the human situation, given its crudity as well as heroism. If life is the raw-material of art, the "unpurged images" have to be purified and rendered into poetry. To get the purged or masterful image, the poet must resort to the mediation of "body" or "symbol." He cannot have a direct access to essence. It must be apprehended only through "symbol" i.e. by analogy to the human condition.

For a man who has lived his life in his poems and who has sought his self through art, living through a long poetic career and facing its traumas and triumphs, must have been a heartbreaking experience. As Yeats approached the end of his poetic life, we find the poetry more and more surcharged with the passion of pain, and a recklessness that comes from setting out for an ideal and finding it, among possible things, most difficult to attain. If unity of being cannot be achieved as long as one is weighed down by the body, it is still an end that cannot be reached except through "body" as via media. In *A Dialogue of Self and Soul*, the soul asks the self to

Fix every wandering thought upon
That quarter where all thought is done[79]

but the self is lost in the contemplation of the consecrated blade, Sato's ancient blade upon its knees. It surmises that the flowering, silken embroidery that is wound round the wooden scabbard must have been torn from some court lady's dress. The soul, on seeing the self thus preoccupied, admonishes it:

Why should the imagination of a man
Long past his prime remember things that are
Emblematical of love and war?
Think of ancestral night that can,
If but imagination scorn the earth
And intellect its wandering
To this and that and t'other thing,
Deliver from the crime of death and birth.[80]

In such a state, the distinction of Is from the Ought, or Knower from the Known would no longer remain. Ironically, however, when the soul thinks of that its tongue becomes stone. A living man may be blind, but if all meaning, either in terms of defeat or victory, is impossible except through the body:

What matter if the ditches are impure?
What matter if I live it all once more?

Since man cannot but live with "that defiling and disfigured shape," what is the good of an escape "if honour find him in the wintry blast?" The poet is content to live it all again and "yet again" even if it be life to pitch "Into the frog-spawn of a blind man's ditch." If the Dialogue appears to end in favour of self or body, it is because Yeats is unwilling, at this stage, to reject the value of body in the enterprise of discovering unified essence in all its nakedness. The soul is tongue-tied when it thinks of the condition beyond the allurements of the physical life. Its advice to the self to fix every wandering thought upon a quarter where thought is transcended falls deaf on its own ears. Yeats is trying to suggest that no direct access to the beatific vision is possible and it is better, in all honesty, to acknowledge the body as valuable no matter how defiled and disfigured a shape one may think it to be. It would be dishonourable and cowardly to give up the struggle now on vain, trivial grounds.

If he has to return, life after life, to enact the daily victory of the unified image, if it is only at such cost that one can achieve Unity of Being or poetic integration, he is content. He will "follow to its source/Every event in action or in thought." A tragically gay acceptance of this human lot wherein man is condemned to make meaning only through the body of the Word is what becomes a measure of the victory won:

> We must laugh and we must sing,
> We are blest by everything,
> Everything we look upon is blest.[82]

Byzantium was written to correct the shortcomings pointed out by Moore in the earlier poem *Sailing to Byzantium*. Moore felt that the poet had contradicted himself by returning to life after rejecting it. In *Byzantium*, a "starlit" or a "moonlit" dome (which in Yeatsian terminology represents the extremity of subjectivity and objectivity), and the Cocks of Hades, "in glory of changeless metal," disdain and scorn aloud

> All that man is,
> All mere complexities,
> The fury and the mire of human veins.[83]

In the first stanza, the poet says: "The unpurged images of day recede." The word "recede" has been used with care. It implies that the impure images of day and of life have only *receded*, not disappeared. One order of reality is merely suspended for a moment. These unpurged images may return again with the appearance of day, a time of rational reality. The cathedral gong that has struck the hour of midnight in the very first stanza, ushering in the night's reign when the soul or the imagination is busy, will resound once again at the end of the poem, tormenting the sea. The hour of midnight is a time-barrier between life and death, the earthly and the spiritual, the active and the contemplative—all opposites. It is a frontier. It is that hour when some revelation is at hand. Apparently, the whole action of the poem takes place between the sounding of the gong around midnight and the next sounding of it—perhaps, sometime in the early hours of the morning, i.e., between midnight and the first crowing of the cock when the spirits which are abroad return to their abode to await another nocturnal tour. As an imaginative enactment in the consciousness of the poet, the poem "happens" when all the agitations of the waking, analytical mind have receded, have been momentarily suspended, and the intuitive eye is opened wide in anticipation of a visionary experience. The "starlit" or "moonlit" dome, representing the two extremes in Yeats's phases of the moon, is a symbol of perfection. As a perfect work of art, it looks down on bungling life and its imperfections. It has been created by a human hand. But it disdains the human now that it has transcended the human and, devoid of imperfections, has become a dateless entity.

In the earlier poem, the speaker was sailing to Byzantium and looking, half-eagerly, and half-scornfully, at the country that is left behind. In this poem, the poet/speaker is already in Byzantium. The poem describes what is taking place in the speaker's consciousness. Having gone through the "agony of flame" in a kind of dance, the speaker has achieved a trance-like state where "all complexities of fury leave." Mounting upon the dolphin, he can now be ferried across the seas of time to a world of purity and timelessness where all creatures must go after necessary purification before re-entering, in due course, the time-bound world again. The dolphin is appropriately used as a ferry en route because it is an amphibian. It belongs equally to "both" worlds. It is at home on land as well as in water. It is, therefore, qualified to take one over the threshold, across time to the opposite shore. It acts as a mediator or synthesizer, helping one through the rites of passage. And, it is by straddling on the dolphin's "mire and blood" that the voyage may be undertaken successfully. It is from the unpurged images that the artifice of eternity can be made, though the artifice may scorn, in its glory of changelessness, the "fury and mire of human veins." Just as it is through the body that one can attain the spiritual essence, through the Word that meaning can be made, it is astraddle the dolphin's "mire and blood" that one can voyage across the seas of time to the purest realms.

Meanwhile, the toil of the smithies of the Emperor who break the "bitter furies of complexities" seems to go on endlessly. The speaker sees that the sea across which he must be taken is gong-tormented. The sea is a meeting-place of vibrations from this world of "mere complexities" and that world beyond time. Towards the end of the poem, those images which had receded appear again. The concluding image is of Life, full of

> Those images that yet
> Fresh images beget
> That dolphin-torn, that gong-tormented sea.

Life has re-appeared more emphatically. The eternal cycle goes on, assimilating the alternating opposites. Once again, in *Byzantium*, Yeats has shown that the only credible unity a poet can achieve is a precariously sustained balance of opposed forces.

Yeats believed that man's life runs its course between extremities till:

> A brand, or flaming breath,
> Comes to destroy
> All those antinomies
> Of day and night;

—the heart calls it "remorse," the body calls it "death."

If Yeats's mind was uneasy with finality it was because finality meant Death. If it is only in Death that the antinomies can be resolved, he must seek to prolong the struggle until the very end. He wanted to believe in a life after death where the conflicts are carried over and replayed because then he could avoid the finality of death.

The poet is not prepared to be a "singer born and lack a theme." There was no remorse in Yeats, no "self-pity for the past, no blindness as to the present":

> Yeats was intensely aware of contemporary thought. His poetry is the outcome of a philosophy which, though he could think towards it only through the medium of the symbol, was yet unified, all detractions reckoned up, by a high and consistent purpose.[84]

Whether one calls it poetic integration or unity of being, either in terms of image-making or self-discovery, Yeats never faltered from his aim. He stopped at nothing in his unflinching quest for truth about himself. If "man is born broken," Yeats has not only the courage to "know completely the incompleteness of life," but also the honesty to accept the limitations of success. He could say at the end of *A Dialogue:*

> When such as I cast out remorse
> So great a sweetness flows into the breast
> We must laugh and we must sing,
> We are blessed by everything,
> Everything we look upon is blest.

This kind of bravery, often verging on rhetoric, shown in the wake of a deep and grave recognition of the futility of human endeavour is not to be regarded as merely an ostentatious gesture used to conceal the dread of personal breakdown. Civilization is brought under a rule, under the semblance of peace by manifold illusion, and history has taught us the lesson that all ancient civilizations—Egyptian, Greek, Roman—were wiped out from the face of the earth. But man's life is thought, and he cannot cease ravening and raging, says Yeats, to come to "the desolation of reality." At one time, his quest for unity threatened to become a heartbreaking frustration but, despite the terror, he held on. The later poetry, especially, is a measure of that unrelenting struggle. The difficulties he had to overcome were many and varied. The East gave him the answer when the Chinamen's "balance" became the ideal for Yeats—a gaiety transfiguring all the dread. The Hermits on Mt. Meru know that "day brings round the night," and "before dawn/ His glory and his monuments are gone." Having received the knowledge of reality and of the tragedy of failure, Yeats Lear-like asks:

> Why should not old men be mad?

With strength of body gone, "here at life's end" he knows that

> Neither loose imagination
> Nor the will of the mind
> Consuming its rag and bone,
> Can make the truth known.[85]

He asks to be granted "an old man's frenzy,"

> Myself must I remake
> Till I am Timon and Lear
> Or that William Blake
> Who beat upon the wall
> Till truth obeyed his call.[86]

His prayer for old age is that he be guarded "from thoughts men think/ In the mind alone." He that "sings a lasting song/ Thinks in a marrow-bone."[87] When certain friends of his expressed astonishment and shock on seeing the old poet write bawdy verse, Yeats was quick to defend himself:

> You think it horrible that lust and rage
> Should dance attendance upon my old age;

They were not such a plague when I was young;
What else have I to spur me into song?[88]

Crazy Jane tells the Bishop, when he advises her to "live in a heavenly mansion/ Not in some foul sty," that "fair and foul are near of kin" when "love hath pitched his mansion in/ The place of excrement."[89] But, in spite of the frenzied, almost reckless, mood of the later poetry, we cannot but see that it is "the same mind," as Blackmur says, "stirring behind the poems on Crazy Jane and the Bishop, on Cuchulain, on Swift, the political poems, the biographical and the doctrinal—a mind that sees the fury and the mire and passion of the dawn as contrary aspects of the real world."[90]

Yeats mastered the technique of making contraries co-exist presenting dramatic conflict in a way as to make the end-product a controlled, moral balance where thought is wedded to feeling. Yeats had the kind of sensibility which could repeat the successes of Donne. Like Donne, a thought to him was an experience. No idea was too strong to violate his mind. Every idea became an image in his mind. His imagination provided verbal equivalents to emotional states of mind.

Yeats wrote *The Circus Animals' Desertion*[91] at a time when his "circus animals" had apparently deserted him. With their desertion, he is deprived (but only for a while?) of the necessary cover or mask that they had provided to work out the changes in his personality. As he enumerates old themes, he asks himself whether the allegorical dreams had not after all been only

Vain gaiety, vain battle, vain repose,
Themes of the embittered heart. . . .

Oisin, Countess Cathleen, Cuchulain, the fool and blind man—all these had been emblematical of "heart mysterious." And yet, when all is said, perhaps it was the dream itself that had enchanted him:

Character isolated by a deed
To engross the present and dominate memory.

Immersed in the preoccupation of the effect the several roles were able to produce, had he forgotten, perhaps, the very purpose behind the invention of the technique of the mask? Had he lost hold over the Self beneath them? True, Yeats like Nietzsche, was more interested in the actor rather than the action, but he could not have lost sight of the man behind all this. He knew that the circus animals,

> Those stilted boys, that burnished chariot,
> Lion and woman and the Lord knows what,

were a mere show that he had put up. By raising the doubt if

> Players and painted stage took all my love,
> And not those things that they were emblems of,

Yeats shows, once again, the rare honesty and courage he had to question his own motives at every stage in order to ensure that his integrity is intact. It is a quality typical of Yeats, a characteristic attitude that even after great bitterness did not desert him. He was man enough to confront the reality.

With the ladder gone, he must return to the "foul rag-and-bone shop of the heart," the "fury and the mire of human veins," "all that man is," "all mere complexities." But if all masterful images have begun from:

> A mound of refuse or the sweepings of a street,
> Old kettles, old bottles, and a broken can,
> Old iron, old bones, old rags, that raving slut
> Who keeps the till,

then the poet's act of "lying down" where all the ladders start cannot be taken as final. It is an artistic but ostentatious gesture. Yeats has not begun to lie down. Those unpurged images, either through miracle (romantic inspiration) or handiwork (the painful perfecting of a line which may take us hours may be), will get purged, and, growing in pure mind, lead once more to masterful images: "Those images that yet/ Fresh images beget." A man who all through his career has battled against warring elements, who has refused to lie down, could not have ended his career by lying down now. Yeats had an indomitable will, and did not permit himself to submit or yield. If he often appears to revel in defeat rather than victory, it is because he saw in "practical failure" a kind of success. For him, in our end lies our beginning. Like the phoenix, he will seek to rebuild life and reconstruct the self, from the ashes, at every instance.

Yeats's whole Poetics is built upon conflict. The aesthetics of quarrel is used to achieve the ethics of balance. If the conflict is resolved at any time, it is only a temporary resolution. A final reconciliation is resisted and, in a sense, put off. That Yeats was still writing poetry on the eve of his death shows how relentlessly he kept up a struggle through all the stages of his life. He never gave up the fight. One wonders if perhaps he included in it, towards the end, even God. He wrote in one of his supernatural songs about man's battles against different kinds of opposition:

> He with body waged a fight,
> But body won; it walks upright.
> Then he struggled with the heart;
> Innocence and peace depart.
> Then he struggled with the mind;
> His proud heart he left behind.
> Now his wars on God begin;
> At stroke of midnight God shall win.[92]

Did he, then, concede defeat before God? However, till the gong strikes "midnight," even if the great stage curtain is about to drop, he will not "break up his lines to weep." Yeats conceived life as tragedy and with "gaiety transfiguring all that dread" it became a "tragic gaiety."

Talking of the hazards of modern poetry, Heller makes some illuminating remarks:

At heart all poetry is praise and celebration. Its joy is not mere pleasure, its lamentation not mere weeping, and its despair not mere despondency. Whatever it does, it cannot but confirm the existence of a meaningful world—even when it denounces its meaninglessness. Poetry means order, even with the indictment of chaos; it means hope, even with the outcry of despair. It is concerned with the true stature of things, all great poetry is realistic.[93]

Heller's remarks find ratification in the poetry of Yeats who faced up to the hazards of modern poetry and emerged triumphant.

Yeats was no idle poetaster. To make his poems, he had broken his life in a mortar as it were. He knew what a sacrifice it had meant to him. He had seen others enjoying life while he stood alone with himself— "commenting, commenting."

For its sake he had buried his youth, and "raised over it a cairn—of clouds" in the hope that someday perhaps he should be articulate. He took his poetry very seriously and believed that art had a moral value. This intense and deeply moral element of Yeats's poetry made it impossible for art not to have an impact on life. His introduction to the Symbolist Movement had come through Symons and Pater but, unlike them, he did not want to place art beyond morality. Like Shelley, he believed that poets were the "unacknowledged legislators of the world." Poetry did make something happen. In his poem *The Man and the Echo,* the speaker asks:

Did that play of mine send out
Certain men the English shot?
Did words of mine put too great strain
On that woman's reeling brain?
Could my spoken words have checked
That whereby a house lay wrecked?[94]

However, the doubts and questions about the morality of art were nothing compared to his deep engagement with the problem of man's place in the world. The personae of his early poetry were shadowy, vague and blurred. To acquire a sharper and strongly defined form, he had turned to a more concrete past—to Irish legendary heroes and historical figures. If he finally turned away from characters borrowed from Irish folklore and moved towards a more direct speech, it was once again the inner compulsion to make man his metaphor that impelled him. Whatever other doubts he may have had, natural to his time and craft, Yeats was never at any time of his life in two minds about this. Quite early he had written: "I'm hunting truth into its thicket and it is my business to keep close to the impressions of sense, to common daily life"[95] To achieve this objective he tried to find "some natural speech, rhythm and syntax, and to set it out in some pattern, so seeming old that it may seem all men's speech."[96]

The search for Unity did not seem an illusionary exercise to him while he was engaged in the struggle to give it poetic form in an integral image. It is true that the beatific vision is denied to man as long as he remains self-conscious about it. But, Yeats found a substitutive solution to this by putting on a variety of roles, whereby he may lose, momentarily, the uneasy burden of the self. Yeats wrote: "Man can embody truth but not know it." Given all the premises, however, he would still not be prevented from embodying it wherever possible. Since all art is "in the last analysis an endeavour to condense as out of the flying vapour of the world an image of human perfection,"[97] he would, if he could not perfect life, at least perfect his art. He would compromise but only by putting his whole life into the poetry so completely that it would no longer have a separate identity from his art. For a man who makes no difference between the two, the poem is not only a paradigm for the possibility of Unity of Being, it is the only paradigm of it. And since, having taken this stance, every power he can command is engaged in perfecting art rather than life, it would be superfluous to look for Unity anywhere except in the poem—in terms of a poetic integration of conflicting impulses. Having achieved it once, in a unified Image, if he is unable to sustain it for long, and has to enact it again, Yeats has shown that he is not content to rest in a single victory. He can repeat the victory again and again a number of times.

It is the tragic fate of every symbolic artist, who awaits the "vision" but does not want to lose either his self-identity or his connections with Man, that he has to return after each successful attempt at a unified Image to the starting point from where he must begin again.

In being "content to live it all again," Yeats has shown not only the courage to plunge into the abyss of his Self but also the final acceptance of reality by not expressing shock at what he sees there, as he looks into the heart of the Real. What does it matter if his every success is only temporary and, therefore, a partial failure. We must accept his achievement in his own terms. And, therefore, we must imagine him content. By the personal struggle inside himself and in his art, Yeats has enacted and dramatized for us the universal mythology of the Self. Like Stephen Dedalus, he will "go to encounter for the millionth time the reality of experience"[98] and forge in the smithy of his soul "the uncreated conscience" of his race.

NOTES

1. Cited from a letter to Katharine Tynan, 14th March, 1888, *Letters,* p. 63.
2. Yeats, *Autobiographies,* p. 470.
3. T.S. Eliot, "Yeats," *Selected Prose,* p. 203.
4. *W.B. Yeats: A Critical Anthology,* ed. Pritchard, pp. 34-35.
5. *Ibid.,* p. 35.
6. Yeats, *Autobiographies,* p. 87.
7. *Ibid.,* p. 470.
8. *W.B. Yeats: A Critical Anthology,* p. 38.
9. *Ibid.*
10. *Ibid.*
11. *Ibid.*

12. Yeats, *Selected Criticism and Prose*, p. 162.
13. Denis Donoghue, *Yeats*, p. 15.
14. Yeats, *CP*, p. 109.
15. *Ibid.*
16. Denis Donoghue, *Yeats*, p. 16.
17. Yeats, *CP*, p. 21.
18. Yeats, *Selected Criticism and Prose*, p. 149.
19. Yeats, *Autobiographies*, p. 472.
20. Yeats, *Selected Criticism and Prose*, pp. 44-45.
21. Yeats, *CP*, pp. 7-8.
22. *Ibid.*, p. 8.
23. *Ibid.*, p. 9.
24. Yeats, *Selected Criticism and Prose*, p. 46.
25. *Ibid.*, p. 49.
26. Brenda S. Webster, *Yeats: A Psychoanalytic Study* (London: Macmillan, 1974), p. 3.
27. David Lynch, *Yeats: The Poetics of the Self* (Chicago: The Univ. of Chicago Press, 1979), p. 200.
28. Yeats, *CP*, p. 35.
29. *Ibid.*, p. 44.
30. *Ibid.*, p. 105.
31. Denis Donoghue, *The Ordinary Universe*, p. 133.
32. *Ibid.*
33. George Wright, *The Poet in the Poem: The Personae of Eliot, Yeats and Pound* (New York: Gordian Press, 1974), p. 90.
34. Yeats, *Autobiographies*, p. 102.
35. Yeats, *CP*, pp. 22-23.
36. *Ibid.*, p. 35.
37. *Ibid.*, p. 42.
38. *Ibid.*, p. 77.
39. *Ibid.*, p. 90.
40. *Ibid.*
41. *Ibid.*, p. 101.
42. *Ibid.*
43. *Ibid.*, p. 241.
44. *Ibid.*, pp. 120-21.
45. Yeats, *Selected Criticism and Prose*, p. 265.
46. Yeats, *Autobiographies*, p. 65.
47. Denis Donoghue, *Yeats*, p. 27.
48. Yeats, *Selected Criticism and Prose*, p. 173.

49. Lillian Feder, *Ancient Myth in Modern Poetry* (Princeton: Princeton Univ. Press, 1971), pp. 61-62.
50. Michael Schmidt, *A Reader's Guide to Fifty Modern British Poets* (New York: Heinemann, 1979), p. 54.
51. Richard Ellmann, *Man and the Masks*, p. 208.
52. Yeats, *CP*, p. 147.
53. A. Alvarez, *The Shaping Spirit: Studies in Modern English and American Poets* (London: Chatto and Windus, 1958), p. 39.
54. Louis MacNeice, *The Poetry of W.B. Yeats* (1941; rpt. New York: OUP, 1969), p. 58.
55. Frank Kermode, p. 6.
56. *Ibid.*, p. 19.
57. Yeats, *CP*, p. 151.
58. *Ibid.*, p. 152.
59. Denis Donoghue, *The Ordinary Universe*, p. 138.
60. Andrew Parkin, *The Dramatic Imagination of W.B. Yeats* (Dublin: Gill and Macmillan, 1978), p. 44.
61. Yeats, *CP*, p. 180.
62. *Ibid.*, p. 182.
63. *Ibid.*, p. 181.
64. *Ibid.*, p. 192.
65. *Ibid.*, p. 217.
66. *Ibid.*, pp. 218-19.
67. *Ibid.*, p. 222
68. *Ibid.*, p. 223.
69. *Ibid.*, p. 224.
70. *Ibid.*, p. 235.
71. *Ibid.*, p. 236.
72. *Ibid.*, pp. 242-43.
73. *Ibid.*, p. 243.
74. *Ibid.*, pp. 244-45.
75. *Ibid.*, pp. 381-82.
76. *Ibid.*, p. 193.
77. *Yeats: A Collection of Critical Essays*, ed. John Unterecker (Englewood Cliffs, New Jersey: Prentice-Hall, 1963), p. 90.
78. Yeats, *CP*, pp. 199-200.
79. *Ibid.*, p. 265.
80. *Ibid.*
81. *Ibid.*, p. 266.
82. *Ibid.*, p. 267.

83. *Ibid.*, p. 280.
84. T.R. Henn, *The Lonely Tower: Studies in the Poetry of W.B. Yeats*, 2nd Edition (1950; rev. London: Methuen, 1965), p. 352.
85. Yeats, *CP*, p. 346.
86. *Ibid.*, p. 347.
87. *Ibid.*, p. 326.
88. *Ibid.*, p. 359.
89. *Ibid.*, p. 295.
90. R.P. Blackmur, "The Later Poetry of W.B. Yeats," in *W.B. Yeats: A Critical Anthology*, p. 129.
91. Yeats, *CP*, pp. 391-92.
92. *Ibid.*, p. 332.
93. Erich Heller, *The Disinherited Mind*, p. 272.
94. Yeats, *CP*, p. 393.
95. Yeats, *Autobiographies*, p. 471.
96. *Ibid.*, p. 532.
97. Cited from Richard Ellmann, *Man and the Masks*, pp. 188-89.
98. James Joyce, *A Portrait of the Artist as a Young Man* (1916; rpt. Middlesex: Penguin Books, 1976), p. 253.

Of Style and the Man

We know that any attempt to restore "original unity" is futile, and yet we despair of its disappearance because it is unity that gives meaning to existence. We accept the loss, but do not, and cannot, give up making effort to regain at least some of the virtues of the "wholeness" that has departed from our consciousness. Withdrawing from one ontological claim to another, we have come to rest upon a retreat from metaphysics to aesthetics—Starting from the deification of Nature to the demythification of the Cosmos, and leading up, as Krieger says, to the mythification of art.[1]

From God's world to the human work of art is a long way, and it has taken many centuries to arrive at it. The transition is from the demythologized *is* to an *as if*. In the final deprivation, only "the word as make-believe remains"[2] for man. If participation as an actual experience is to be discovered by our "islanded consciousness," it has to be done by "special exertion."[3] This is where "'Imagination' in the genial or creative sense of the word"[4] comes in, with its power to diffuse but so as to unite into a single perception. If the poet can remake nature and himself anew, the word that was "first spoken by God may eventually be respoken by man."[5]

Coleridge said that by imitating nature in his finite mind, the artist can bring the object back to life. But the imitation of an "idol" would become a "purely technical" process unless the artist relies on the "life inherent" in the object he imitates. The work of art in positing unity projects unity *as if* it were there. Though semantic and imagistic, it is the only thing left from earlier retreats. And even this word-made-form "can no longer create more than a visionary reality"[6] that we all accept as fiction. So, the reality created by the artist is fictional, as all our realities are in the final analysis—only illusionary. The greater our eagerness to grasp reality or understand it, the more it appears elusive. However, if fancy is a "deceiving elf," it offers at least a momentary respite from the "weariness, the fever, and the fret"[7] of life. If artistic reality is "ideal," it is not for that reason "unreal." It is the consistent dream, giving continuity where there is none. As dream, it remains undefeated.

The pre-romantic assumption had been that the real self of man may be discovered in interaction with the outside world, in its "combat with circumstances," since the self man projected in public life appeared as though stripped of private inhibitions. The romantics realized how superficial this assumption was. They sought to discover the real self alone in Nature. But despite their best efforts, even a Wordsworth could not sustain and uphold that prelapsarian self. In his *The Prelude* he says, "There *was* a boy: ye knew him well, ye cliffs/ And islands of Winander!"[8]—already the boy has become past tense. The ideal was presented by Wordsworth but even he found it impossible to embody it. In spite of Colerdige's ideal poet who brings the "whole soul of man into activity," the claim of unity in a well-made poem itself may be questionable. The problem, in fact, is not a modern one. Each age is equidistant from Arcadia and every poet must face the Orphic predicament or invent a new arcadia of his own. Today's man is never less alone than when alone. There is no longer one self. There is a personality made up of many selves. One must wear consciously the mask of many selves if one hopes to discover the real self.

Every attempt at integration may prove to be futile unless we agree to accept the momentariness of the integration achieved by the poet in any single poem. Quite surprisingly, however, in accepting the vulnerability of the self and the fragility of the Unity he posits, the modern poet has not lost but gained in confidence. As the last Romantic, Yeats was aware of the precarious quality of the unity he sought to embody. Perhaps, if he had not been plagued by doubts and uncertainties, he would not have resorted to the use of irony, mask, conflict, etc. He was worried about how one may make one's claim to unity without it appearing too facile. Yeats's dialectic was a way of recovering "radical innocence" by voluntarily and deliberately inventing it. The nostalgia for the golden age of original unity was turned into an aesthetic.

Impersonalization was the method of Eliot. Distancing himself from the self, ostensibly repudiating lyrical poetry, was perhaps a camouflage. One cannot define impersonality except in terms of personality. It was a decentring from the *centre*. In essence, there is not much difference between the personal poetry of Yeats, and Eliot's profession of impersonality. MacNeice points out that while in their "critical utterances they are often diametrically opposed, poetry appearing essentially impersonal to one and personal to the other; in practice all that this amounts to is that Eliot avoids saying 'I'."[9] When he could not go any farther, Eliot fell back on Christianity. But the "centre of the world is not the place where the religious word is manifest,"[10] nor can it be found in Pound's hierarchical order. Yeats learned that the poet cannot rely on the "life inherent in the words he uses."[11] With a split between sound and meaning, phenomena and name have been estranged. To restore the "participation mystique," Yeats sought to "draw the life forth from within himself."[12] Each poem is loaded with irony, an irony that does not obtrude because it is assimilated into the idiom of conflict that he uses in poems like *Sailing to Byzantium*.

Yeats was aware of the "spider-like plight of the modern artist, forced to spin everything out of his guts."[13] He knew that the artist must plumb the depths within if he is to find any answers. This can, however, put an undue strain on the poet's role and creative instinct. Where "nothing is given, everything begins and ends with him, and his job becomes proportionately more difficult, tentative, compromising, risky,"[14] leading not so much to a "crisis of style" as a "crisis of no-style," or a "crisis of nerve."

The new romantic theory asks us to look for the nature-spirits within ourselves. A Wordsworth sought to experience "dis-godded" nature by a nostalgic return to original participation in terms of a pantheistic outlook. Our twentieth-century problem is that "Pan has shut up shop. But he has not retired from business; he has merely gone indoors."[15] Perhaps if poets like Larkin, Berryman and Lowell showed in their work a self-conscious "admission of defeat by the wörld and a withdrawal from it," it was because living in a world which had lost its centre, they lacked the confidence of a Yeats who, having been brought up in a relatively simpler world—man and nature still in communion—did not only "remake himself" but "along the same lines and for the same reasons turned all about him into a legend."[16]

Yeats professed that "Out of the quarrel with ourselves we make poetry." His "distinction between the perfection that is from a man's combat with himself and that which is from a combat with circumstance"[17] would have been inconceivable for many other writers of the twentieth century. For them, division is "between the self they discover and the world they implicitly reject in so doing."[18] A quarrel with the self which poetry has generated, and out of which poetry is made would be unthinkable for them. Yeats's strength came from a deep confidence in the role of the poet and in the notion of the complete man.

For Yeats, unity in terms of analogy to the human situation became the only valid manner of achieving final participation in the absence of original unity. If the imagination is employed systematically and intelligently, its answer to the question of a primary loss of the medieval world-view would be to experience nature as a representation of Man. An imminent danger may be that, in making Man representative of nature, we might drain him of spirit. We have to learn to see man as the microform of the macrocosm if we are to avoid expressing a personality that is purely subjective in orientation. Like Coleridge's "poet," the systematic use of the imagination that Steiner advocated involves the whole man. The poet as creator, in saving the appearances of nature, reverts not to original unity, which may be impossible, but to final participation—the ability to experience the representations as idols (or Images) and then to be able also "to perform the act of figuration consciously, so as to experience them as participated."[19]

In seeking to bring opposing elements together into a tension without making a conscious choice, Yeats was rejecting the duality of a non-participating consciousness which thinks in terms of an "either-or." The existentialist notion that freedom lies "less in our power to choose than to *choose* to choose, in the respect that the primal and original choice determines a *style* of choosing, and the style is the man himself,"[20] may be compared with Yeats's own views. For Yeats, "choosing" was a way of defining one's self and life. The past does not constrain the present if one chooses what portion of that past one wants to inherit, making it relevant to one's present and future. In each choice that one makes, one does not merely choose a specific course of action. In *Essays and Introductions*, Yeats wrote:

> I think my style is myself. I might have found more of Ireland if I had written in Irish but I have found a little, and I have found all myself.[21]

If it took Yeats a lifetime to decide which style to choose, it took him a whole life to make himself as well. The style and the man were inextricably intertwined. In its being a choice that would determine the style of the whole course of one's life, it was an ethic as well as an aesthetic of choosing. Yeats did not appear to be too eager to bring such a complex issue to a final resolution before he was morally and artistically prepared for it. As it was closely related to the making of the Self, his poetics became one of not only self-knowledge but also self-creation. No choice was an isolated episode. Each new choice altered, if ever so slightly, all previous choices. All the previous choices had to be integrated to each new choice to form a whole. No single choice could be evaluated as right or wrong from the moral point of view because it could not be viewed in isolation. Each was only one "ingredient in a tapestry of choices that add up an entire life."[22] There is an "implicit, almost categorical imperative binding upon us at every moment, to so choose that the form of life the choice implies is one we would be willing to live always."[23] In Yeats's case, also, the problem lay in having to choose a life one "would be willing to live always." This partly explains why Yeats considered very important the decision he took to revise his earlier poems and order his poetic life.

The poetic integration that Yeats wanted to achieve was one that comprehended all the stages, carrying the previous stage into the next one without discarding it. To decide between two choices—as "either-or"—was unacceptable. His was a dipolar view, an "either *and* or" or "both-and" way of looking at things. The poem could become a dialectical structure in which "resolved or unresolved problems" consume their multiplicity in the unity of its form, as in *Sailing to Byzantium, Irish Airman, Byzantium* and *Among School Children.* Often, as in the case of Eliot and Yeats, "a writer's entire development may form a dialectical unity,"[24] the whole being embodied in the part, and the part in the whole.

Though as an "authentic" modern Yeats felt deeply the lack of a tradition or belief to hold on to, he did not permit himself to fail as an artist. The absence of a coherent system, religion or philosophy did not seem to daunt him. It only afforded a greater challenge to him. Denied the more obvious forms of belief, Yeats made his art itself the central focus of all value. Above all, he believed in his art. What separates the contemporary artist from his predecessor is the lack of any external standard by which to measure the reality of his world. As a poet seriously committed to his art, he has not only "to launch his craft and control it," but also to "make his own compass."[25] "A lesser poet," says Holroyd, commenting on Yeats's resilience in some of the most trying of situations, "lacking an established tradition, would have been spoilt by dabbling in theosophy and occultism, but for Yeats poetry always came first."[26] He was not seeking truths to incorporate into his poetry. He wanted to ascend to truth through poetry. Only a man who had made his life an "artifice of eternity" can do that. To begin with, he must make of his life a drama, accepting Style and Gesture as stylizations of this life. As a poet in the "tradition of the self," style was as important in life as in art. He says in *Autobiographies:*

> I can only set up a secondary or interior personality created out of the tradition of myself, and this personality (alas, only possible to me in my writings) must be always gracious and

simple. It must have that slight separation from interests which makes charm possible, while remaining near enough for passion.[27]

There are several reasons for creating the Self. The artist can "escape from the hot-faced bargainers and the money-changers"[28] whose morals are different from his own. He can also extend his own and the reader's experience. Yeats differed from the early romantic poet who expressed "a self that already exists"[29] and recorded merely pre-existing experiences. The poet who has created a tradition of the self in a "man of action whose deeds are his poems."[30] He combines in himself both the active and the contemplative man.

The artist seeks to escape the transient and changing forms of life by transforming himself into something outside nature and, therefore, outside change. The work of art could become a ground where both worlds meet, one in which we live and the other which we cannot occupy. The poet in *Sailing to Byzantium* is poised between two worlds—one which he has left behind, and the other which he must enter but which he still has not wholeheartedly accepted. The work the poet creates is born from and in the world of the senses but it is not of it—like the dome of *Byzantium.* When the poet expresses an emotion that belongs to life, his aim is to put a life-experience into words. The words are "the emotion metamorphosed." The poetic word transforms reality, does not represent it. The words are fragments of "reality given verbal embodiment."[31] This is true of all poetry. Yeats's case was different because when an artist lives his life in his poems, when his "deeds" are his poems, reality and its verbal embodiment become inseparable.

What marked Yeats out from other poets of his time was a vivid sense of reality. To seek reality was almost a passion for him. In his relentless search for truth, embodying it wherever he could, he even invented "several roles" to widen the range of his vision. They were meant to take him closer to reality. This is not the reality of the philosopher. Yeats's poetry is not a mere philosophical quest for truth. It is reality seen not from a distance, as something notional, but experienced in identity with its idea—the image and idea reconciled.

Yeats was highly conscious of his vocation as a poet. A serious commitment to the life of a poet made him almost bardic towards the end. The prophetic tone of the later poetry is the bard's voice, the voice of a man who has seen, though perhaps momentarily, the face of truth. The quest for identity was "authentic," but fraught with hazards. Theosophy, the Occult, the Masks—all these were tried out as means of coming closer to the truth. Whatever may have been the means, the end they sought to achieve was a fuller realization of the Self.

We are all ready to agree that myths and, correspondingly, masks used as metaphors are important structures that give shape and definition to art. They concretize the abstract. But we sometimes think that to employ them is too deliberate an act to be called "sincere." There is no critical unanimity regarding the technique an artist ought to use in handling the tools at his disposal. If he is to make "authentic" his voice and vision, he ought not to, we feel, be unduly concerned about "device." The use of myth or mask makes him less sincere as a poet. He should write as a "man speaking to men," without an intermediary figure or agency. If, as Barfield says, sincerity has become a rather "ticklish problem" it is because people have begun to acknowledge a "something in themselves" which cannot be identified either with their deepest or strongest emotions. And this is the "malaise" which has been "creeping over the whole world of literature since the decline of Romanticism."[32]

The rather simplified view of the early centuries that a person is judged by the station he occupies—his style of speech and manner reflective of the man—no longer holds. The nineteenth-century romanticists had no faith in this one-to-one correspondence. They suspected that in fact the opposite was true. The real man was not to be discovered in his social surroundings. There he was play-acting a role expected of him. To find the real man, one must leave him alone in Nature—reflecting, musing, recollecting. Not "decorum" but sincerity was valued in Romantic Literature. The romantics projected the self in art and, to that extent, blurred the distinction between life and art. The "persona" of the work of art could be identified with the poet's personality. The Victorian persona of Browning's poetry was a character as unlike the poet as possible but, nevertheless, completely identified with him. The situation is different today. The real self must be discovered through a mask/persona. As Bradbury points out, in the "theatre of our modern international existence, with all the pleasure of theatre, and all its anxiety, as facades crumble, experiences dissolve, and we look into the self to find there just another actor. For we live, after all, in a time when the theatrical display of multiple styles is an essential term or condition of our modern and increasingly self-doubting existence."[33] It is for this reason that Gesture, Manner and Style became modes of expression in Yeats's poetry. Against the Victorian method, Yeats posited a different kind of poem. "Personal Utterance, which has almost ceased in English Literature could be as fine an escape from rhetoric and abstractions as drama itself," he said. The poet writes most truthfully about himself when he is writing about what he is not—his anti-self. The self is defined in terms of its opposite. When Oscar Wilde says that "All bad poetry springs from genuine feeling,"[34] he does not mean that most genuine feeling is a dull feeling, nor even that genuine feeling needs the mediation of artifice if it is to be transfigured into good poetry. What Wilde is trying to suggest is that the direct public expression of a feeling does not necessarily yield the truth. It is likely, instead, to pervert it. We cannot get at the real self without a certain amount of role-playing. A poet needs to distance or depersonalize himself. He needs a Mask. If we look back at the Romantics, we wonder if the self they projected was not, after all, in its autobiographical associations, an artistic invention. Was not, the self of the Romantic Poet itself an artificial construction?

The concept of persona stays, but our understanding of the relationship between the poem, the poet and the reader has to be redefined. Though the "stream of consciousness" technique aimed at a realistic approach, it dissolved the "contours" of character, blocking entry into that central being called "self." The mythical method preconceives a mask, creating character to fit it. In the new idea of identity, art places a deliberate emphasis on artifice.

Parallel to the Christian myth of the Fall is the romantic myth of a fall into self-consciousness. Poetry replacing religion, as Arnold anticipated, can deliver us from self-consciousness by recapturing unself-conscious experience through the poet's capacity to overthrow all burdens and sing in "unpremeditated," "full-throated ease." The poet may recover "radical innocence" through ritual—Yeats's "dying into a dance"—and the magical operation of the word. The "conception of poetry as magic implies," Paz says, "an aesthetic of action."[35] Art is an "intervention in reality," not merely a representation of it. It mirrors the world but the mirror is magical, and it changes the world. As Wallace Stevens writes:

> They said, "You have a blue guitar,
> You do not play things as they are."
> The man replied, "Things as they are
> Are changed upon the blue guitar."[36]

It is doubtful if poetry would survive without metaphor, analogy being the only way of relating ourselves to the phenomena around us. Without the mediation of metaphor, it would not be possible to write poetry at all. It is only through symbol or analogy that "participation" is possible for us today. The poet would be accused of projecting a purely subjective vision if he did not conceal himself, as Yeats did, under the guise of some character or voice. Brooks rightly felt there is a "danger that Yeats's conception of art throws the poet too much back onto himself and thus risks committing him to a morbid subjectivity."[37] Fortunately, Yeats's masks helped him to overcome this risk and preserve his poetic integrity. But for the rhetoric of the Mask, he might indeed have put his integrity at stake. His dramatic stage is peopled with characters representing contrary views, and yet each voice surprises us with its authentic tone. If the voices of life, the body and self, as against those of art, the spirit and soul, sounded more passionate and had a greater right of truth, it is because Yeats was always a man devoted to his art but an artist committed to life. The sincerity lay in his never forfeiting his claims to either.

It is concern for the critical dilemma of the artist, who, even while desiring to be sincere, cannot speak directly in his own voice, that prompted Oscar Wilde to make some seemingly paradoxical statements on the subject. "Create yourself," Wilde said, and "be yourself your pose." Wilde thought "insincerity" made one more attractive and interesting. A "man is least himself when he talks in his own person. Give him a mask and he will tell you the truth."[38]

Conflicts get resolved in the process of writing out one's thoughts since one has to necessarily discriminate the crude from the relatively finer emotions. What distinguishes the poet is the degree of intensity and the quality of the sensibility that judges and selects and creates artefacts. For this, form and style may be all-important to the artist. Style is "the playing of strength when the day's work is done, a secret between a craftsman and his craft,"[39] and inseparable from his nature, says Yeats. It is, as Lentricchia writes, "the victory over the tragic, that glitters in the eye described in 'Lapis Lazuli'."[40]

In *Lapis Lazuli* Yeats relates the idea of identity-making to the principle of repetition—like the ritual dance of the Dancer whose agony of trance is an agony of flame that cannot singe a sleeve—and leads it up to "tragic gaiety." The tragedy we now experience is neither less nor more, the poet implies, than what others have experienced, what Hamlet and Lear knew. It is the tragedy of a single "archetypal" character—something that *all* men aim at, find and lose. This historical pattern gives a kind of continuity to civilization:

> All things fall and are built again,
> And those that build them again are gay.

There is something tragicomic about the scene. The glittering eyes of the Chinamen, "'mid many wrinkles," are gay. Their acceptance is based not on ignorance but on knowledge. The self faces the world not in fear but in confidence. As a twentieth-century romantic, Yeats reinforced the self's freedom by relating it to *Culture and Style*. The self is neither opposed to culture nor to style. It is itself a cultural achievement, a stylistic triumph. Style is "the glitter in the eye" described in *Lapis Lazuli*. The sheer intensity of tragedy makes way for the comic so that the ultimate vision is, as in the last plays of Shakespeare, tragicomic. It is tragic gaiety transfiguring all the dread.

It is "style" that transfigures life. Since Yeats believed that "the self-conquest of the writer who is not a man of action is style," he "persistently worked at the task of forming a style which would be a fit vehicle for his 'personal Utterance'."[41] We get some idea of what meaning Yeats gave to sincerity if we recall his words: "All that is personal soon rots; it must be packed in ice and salt."[42]

In *Among School Children*, as the poet/speaker walks through the long schoolroom questioning, he sees himself as the children see him—the sixty-year-old smiling public man is very different from the man he thinks he is. The irony, of course, is directed against him. It is better, he says, to smile on all that smile and show "There is a comfortable kind of old scarecrow."

The children remind him of Maud Gonne, and he wonders if "she stood so at that age." Her memory drives the heart wild as it recalls what a beautiful woman she had been. Her present image, juxtaposed against his sixty-year-old-smiling-public-man one, is a "mess of shadows." Where, in all these changes, is the real person? Both nuns and mothers worship images. Those that "keep a marble or a bronze repose," though different from those that animate a mother's dreams, also break hearts. It is only in the "Presences" which combine all passion, piety and affection into a single Image—nature and art, dancer and dance identified—that we find labour blossoming. In the intense moment, all change is momentarily transfixed. It is that Unity of Being where "all the nature murmurs in response if but a single note be touched."[43] The unity is experienced only momentarily because "the instantaneous is the purest, most intense form of time."[44] The bird of *Byzantium*, in being wrought "out of nature," is past change. But its changelessness is earned at the cost of lifelessness. Its perfection is a denial of existence and the infinite possibility of being. Its lasting perfection is tasteless. Intensity is better than Eternity. So, there is value even in the momentariness of momentous experience of harmony—a moment when all discordance melted. Time appears to have come to a standstill:

> My body of a sudden blazed;
> And twenty minutes more or less
> It seemed, so great my happiness,
> That I was blessed and could bless.[45]

To recreate the momentous experience in the reader, the poet invents an "objective correlative." His poem is successful if the "objective analogue" elicits in the reader a proper or analogous response. Mask and rhetoric become stylistic ropetricks upon which to hold in balance the meaning of the poem.

If all art is artifice, where is sincerity to be found? What should a poet who wants to validate his voice do in this ironic situation? Yeats reconciled himself to this problem in an interesting way. Since a fiction could never be mistaken for one's self, behind the fiction of being a fiction, one could be oneself without being attacked. The "mask" would provide an added advantage since one could wear not only the mask of one's self but also the mask of the anti-self which comes only to those "who are no longer deceived, whose passion is reality."[46]

Yeats associated sincerity with passion, an emotional attitude. From struggle, conflict is generated, and conflict may bring with it self-realization. Richard Ellmann says that Yeats had the quality of speaking "from different poles of his being," and Whitmanlike contradicting himself.[47] The many selves are multiplications or divisions of the self of the poet. If there is no resolution of the conflict, and ultimate unity is attainable only at rare moments, there is, nevertheless, something to exult in—the occasionable triumph wrought out of meaninglessness and confusion. In the knowledge that

> Whatever flames upon the night
> Man's own resinous heart has fed[48]

there is the confident assertion of man's power. Man can give aesthetic form even to a morally chaotic experience. In the search for reality, defeat or surrender to the tragic has no place. The poet's aim must be to bring all things into unity by a mood—a unity that is not static but "alive and glowing like a star, all in harmony with himself."

Yeats's adoption of the mask was related to the search for reality. It was the

> poet plumbing the depths of his own nature in so powerful an effort of inner observation, that he lays hold of the potential in the real, and takes up what nature has left as a mere outline or sketch in his soul in order to make of it a finished work of art.[49]

The creation of many selves was an attempt to explore the potentiality of the real, and discover the true self. Therefore the standards we use to judge sincerity in ordinary life cannot be used in judging a poet and his work. Aesthetics calls for a deeper morality at the personal level—the kind of which Polonius, in Shakespeare's *Hamlet,* spoke: To thine own self be true, and it must follow, as the night the day, thou canst not then be false to any man.

The kind of sincerity that becomes a measure of a poet's integrity may perhaps be related to "authenticity" as defined by Irving Howe. He says that authenticity is a repudiation of "bad faith." It asserts the self as absolute. Howe distinguishes sincerity from authenticity. While we are "persuaded" toward sincerity, we are "stripped, shocked and shamed into authenticity." If we assess Yeats's work on the basis of the distinction made by Howe, his creation of multiple selves, however contradictory, cannot be set aside as merely rhetorical devices to hide the real self. They are the many facets of the one self, seeking its authenticity in muitiple voices. In striding over ordinary moral considerations, Yeats was trying to be faithful to his poetic "swadharma," and re-affirming the existentialist assertion that "Man is nothing else but that which he makes of himself."[50] If after knowledge of the freedom of the self to make itself, he struggles to become what he ought to be, and not what he is or wants to be, it would be an example of "bad faith." In expressing its freedom to make itself, Yeats's self defines itself always in terms of what it is not, leaving one with what "is." The formal gesture of stripping his self of the "embroidered coat of mythologies" was a repudiation of ornamentation, and a determination to encounter the authentic and naked self. After every stage is completed, it is simply a question of shedding yet another new accretion in preference for one's own self—starting with role-playing and ending up with role-shedding. If in the intimacy of encounter, the authentic self reveals not one but two faces—self and daimon—it is because the two are facets of the one self. It follows as a kind of corollary that a poetry, which attempts to discover this self becomes an aesthetic of contraries. The artist performs a dual function. While the man in him is a participator, as artist he is also a spectator of the human scene. But as spectator, his voice carries no personal conviction. He must invent a character that would help him to perform both functions without putting too great a strain on either. To make his self convincing to others, he may choose a language that is natural as well as dramatic, making one feel "the presence of a man thinking and feeling." Yeats believed that the essence of genius lay in precision—that "life where passion and thought are one." The ideal that, according to him, distinguishes great poetry characterizes his own idea of personality— "a man brought into unity by a mood." What mood is to personality, style is to poetry.

Every exercise Yeats engaged in was related, as Brooks says, to the one dominating principle—the search for reality and unity:

> Contemplation, solitude, wrestling with the dark angel of one's anti-self, all of these were for Yeats ways of getting back to ultimate reality.[51]

By using images as general and striking as,

> Hearts with one purpose alone
> Through summer and winter seem
> Enchanted to a stone
> To trouble the living stream,[52]

the most personal impressions on the Easter Rising acquire significance in the larger context of a political scenario." Enchanted to a stone" implies that a misguided and partial understanding can drive one to the fanatical pursuit of a single purpose to the exclusion of everything else, thereby obstructing, like a huge stone in midstream, the flow and movement of life.

With maturity, Yeats's different techniques gathered strength and purpose. His aim had been to revive the ancient Irish tradition and folklore. But he discovered that instead of trying to resuscitate that tradition, it would be better to create one that would be distinctly his own. From then onwards, he began to invent characters and build up his own private mythology. The mask that had earlier served as a defensive armour to protect one's self became the anti-self. The anti-self, being an exact opposite, was an ideal he would try to live up to. If the unconscious and dark forces within oneself are made conscious in order to be integrated to the self, wearing the mask of the anti-self would not only engender conflict but also help to complete the "partial mind." He deliberately "forced moments of crisis upon himself, pitted one aspect of himself against another, of his whole self against some challenging aspect of the external world."[53] The struggle deepened his self-knowledge. It must have required an extraordinary strength of will to be able to give up the easier way of speaking in a single voice, and substitute it with the difficult and strenuous one of living constantly in a state of "fitful uncertainty."

The mask was not simply a means of avoiding the necessity of finding a single satisfactory solution. It embodies the poet's determination to exploit all the possibilities of life. "No pattern sufficed him for long" since he found each "too forcible an arrest of the changing world." Therefore, in "the light of new experience every formulation had to be destroyed and a new one attempted."[54]

As a Romantic, Yeats felt strongly the limitations of ordinary experience, and the masks were one way of compensating for it. To that extent, they are, even in their diversity, his own voices, not merely stylistics adaptations. If technique and mask had been ends in themselves he would not have moved away from the symbolic tradition which lured many writers of his time with its aspiration to create an Ideal world. The symbolist influence, while it was strong, tried to draw him into its world of beauty. But Yeats did not rest there for long. He knew that art can achieve the kind of perfection that will always elude us in life. In spite of this awareness, he stubbornly stuck to *life* and remained loyal to the human situation. It is remarkable to see a poet, so committed to his art, proving to be such a fierce defender of life. It appeared as if he preferred defeat in the struggle with life to success in art—art which would remain, in the final analysis, only remotely connected with life's mutability.

Writing a poem like *Sailing to Byzantium,* the poet may have felt exhilarated at the prospect of combining the best of both worlds. But the euphoria would not have lasted long. Like Keats's Cold Pastoral, the Golden Bird fails to respond to "breathing human passion." It will not be able to share the beauty of consummation or the pain of isolation, either fulfilment or the anguish of separation. Cut off from life, Yeats's bird feels an inner impulse to return to it. If the poem is taken as persona, we might say that the poet, having participated in the unity that is the poem, would have felt on stepping out of the poem remote, dislocated and separate from his own creation—every poem an epitaph. Auden wrote of Yeats: "You were silly like us. Your gift survived it all." The art outlives the man who surrenders to the "supersession of breath."

Yeats may have felt that though the perfection of form whose author he was—a perfection achieved out of the imperfection that man is—marked man's triumph over the limitations of his nature, it was a perfection which, once reached, would elude his grasp, even deny him. In its new identity, his own creation, like the "starlit or a moonlit dome" (an apex of perfection) of *Byzantium,* would disdain him, and

> All that man is,
> All were complexities,
> The fury and the mire of human veins.

The poet may have found it difficult to reconcile himself to a situation in which the organic unity and the perfection of form that he authored could disdain him. Though the poem partook of the life of the poet, in its having been born of him, *he* did not have a share in its perfection. This truth would have had a disturbing effect. In the Bird's celebration of life, singing of "What is past, or passing, or to come," the poet may have sought to strike a balance against the disequilibrium of life and art. If what is achieved at the end of *Sailing to Byzantium* appears to be an ironic balance wherein opposing forces are precariously poised against each other, it is, nevertheless, an achieved or "earned" balance, not something merely stated.

Yeats may have felt the futility of achieving something at the cost of giving up life in exchange. He knew that what is temporally attainable in life, art can embody spatially as well. This made his demands on life even greater. He wanted to show that man as creator can build a mirror-resembling dream, a translunar paradise. There are other beginnings possible. The artist is greater than his art. He can repeat the act of unity, even better his performance each time, only he needs art to give life's temporal unity a spatial continuum. The "Presences" may mock man's enterprise since "images" that keep a marble or a bronze repose also break hearts. But if labour is blossoming, what matter if a "line may take us hours maybe" if it *seem* a moment's thought?

It was important for Yeats to maintain, even from the heights, a link with the physical. As Holroyd says, the "man who wishes to remain a poet cannot sever himself from the human, however strong may be his inclination towards the divine."[35] The saint may be the solution to the Outsider's problem but that straight path is not for a poet. Yeats chose the eagle's way, the spiral path. He could never have become a mystic in the sense that Blake was one. Still, he did leave behind something valuable, and his own:

> a record of the struggles, creative and stimulating in themselves, of a scrupulously honest human mind engaged in an heroic endeavour to know reality, and of those other struggles suffered by a representative modern man who would establish "Unity of Being" within himself in despite of the world.[56]

By tenaciously holding on to the Dionysian as against the Apollonian, he was deliberately choosing the tragic mode as against the "ethical." Holroyd sums it up well:

> The truly heroic figure expresses the pathos as well as the nobility of human existence; fully conscious of his own morality and the impermanence of the world, he yet wins through to affirmation. The saint and the mystic having transcended the world of becoming, which is that of human life, automatically cast the pathetic from themselves and therefore are not heroic.[57]

If what is achieved in Yeats's poetry is an ironic balance, it is because, in that vast desolation of reality, Yeats insisted on seeing man heroically fighting against the odds of life and transcending its given limitations.

Though the poetry of dialogue was essential in order to be able to continue the struggle of the self and the anti-self, it had also an interest outside the poetry. The findings of his occult study revealed that man's conscious and unconscious minds represent opposites, and the way to individuation consists in coming to terms with the existing tension between the two. Yeats was trying to find, Robert Langbaum points out, "the link between a man's life and art at that unconscious level where artifice is the agency of the deepest self-expression, and expression carried on through the rituals and the symbols that art and the occult have in common."[58] Both his occult studies and poetry meet at this point. In fact, none of Yeats's interests was redundant to his poetic practice. An artist whose passion is reality would plunge into any experience if it had the one virtue that it could take him closer to his goal. A strong predilection for the Self, and an unrelenting urge to find out the truth about it and the world with which it interacts, is typical of the Romantic. Yeats wrote in one of his letters— "all our art is but the putting our faith and the evidence of our faith into words or forms." For a man who breathed his faith, and staked his all in his poetry,

> the created work of art may become an aspect of the creator's self; it may express the deepest longings and aspirations of the self; it may communicate the insights achieved and it may depict the various states of the self.[59]

When the Unity informs every element in a poem—something posited and hypothesized to derive meaning—and directs the inner telos of the poem, it is not just a virtual mover but a real one. At the meeting point of the self, the persona and the reader, each conferring and eliciting value from the poem, the unity would go beyond the verbal and imagistic level. Overcoming the "semantic surface," it would work a transition from "unity-as-idea" to "unity-as-being." Given the nature of antinomies, no satisfactory thematic resolution may be possible. Conflict would go on perennially. At the level of the poem, a formal, metaphysical, intuitive unity may be temporarily achieved.

To move from "unity-as-idea" to "unity-as-being" means beginning with semantic scanning and proceeding to see the soul of the poet. One would have to constantly move from the poet to the poem, and from the poem to the poet. The poem would become a heuristic strategy to discover the possibilities of the self. It may also become a poetic epiphany. In the epiphanic moment of experience, the poet may have an intuitive apprehension of unity. The unity would last till he steps out of the poem's field of action, completing it. If in the history of its life, the poem is able to re-create, in the good and intelligent reader, the required experience, it would have sufficiently validated the purpose of its creation. By repeating in himself the poet's experience, the reader makes the poem "incarnate in history." At the centre where the poet, reader and poem/persona meet, the distinctions between the poet's soul and semantic surface of the poem get dissolved, and unity becomes present as being.

Unless the poet is able to intuit the unity in the creation of an image, his unity will be like the intellectual unity of the Metaphysical Poet—a "perilous one, wrested by his own effort from a world of incongruities."[60] Yeats saved himself from the danger of a merely intellectual unity by passionately standing at both sides of the borderline in alternation. In that way he could assimilate both the desirable and undesirable, the sacred and the profane. Only a man who has plunged into the abyss of the self, come face to face with the "interior Lucifer," could have written of the varied aspects of human life with the honesty and courage that Yeats did. From a duel with good and evil forces, came self-knowledge. Self-knowledge made him a tragic character. With tragedy came wisdom. Wisdom turned all into a tragic gaiety. Tragic gaiety transfigured the dread of the ultimate fate of man into an affirmation of his true greatness and grandeur. Seen from this point of view, life does not fail the artist. It begets fresh images continually. Its inexhaustible resourcefulness enables him to defy the futility of human endeavour in the creation of an imaginative self that is heroic and undefeated. What life gives, art can transform into a permanent monument of its victory.

There is another way of achieving Unity of Being. Instead of standing on both sides alternatively, which keeps one in a state of "fitful uncertainty," one could stand on the threshold or borderline itself. The cartesian ideal that Yeats had before him was an "either, or" way of looking at things. Chinese inclusiveness is represented in the Bah-kua. The kind of unified vision the Hindu mind put forward includes everything by excluding everything.

In *Sailing to Byzantium,* the speaker is one who, while appearing to be on either side in alternation, is standing at the threshold and contemplating the potentialities of both sides. From that point, both can be viewed in a double vision, as it were, and with equal justice. Though bred in the western tradition, Yeats showed that the poetic integration he sought to achieve was distinctly unconventional. On the surface, the poet rejects one world for another. But, the apparent rejection of any one element only serves to highlight what is not rejected. It is not so much a rejection as a selection of those elements which he wanted to constitute his life and art. The rejection is a conscious and deliberate act. It is meant to affirm what is not rejected. One is made acutely aware of the presence of what is absent. Its absence is strikingly felt because one genuinely expected a presence. Therefore, because of the ostensible act of rejection, the rejected is put into finer focus, and subtly brought back in through the back-door. In the final analysis, therefore, it appears as if Yeats has not wholeheartedly rejected anything at all. This is perhaps Yeats's special version of the Hindu "inclusion" by negation. The poet still aims at bringing all things into an inclusive vision.

NOTES

1. Murray Krieger, *Theory of Criticism: A Tradition and its System* (1976; rpt. Baltimore: The Johns Hopkins Univ. Press, 1981), p. 189.
2. *Ibid.*, p. 190.
3. Owen Barfield, *Saving the Appearances*, p. 89.
4. *Ibid.*
5. *Ibid.*, p. 127.
6. Murray Krieger, *Theory of Criticism*, p. 190.
7. John Keats, "Ode to a Nightingale," Edward Leeson, p. 347.
8. *Ibid.*, p. 300.
9. MacNeice, *The Poetry of W.B. Yeats*, p. 190.
10. Octavio Paz, p. 125.
11. Owen Barfield, p. 129.
12. *Ibid.*
13. Cleanth Brooks, *A Shaping Joy: Studies in the Writer's Craft* (London: Chatto and Windus, 1970), pp. 118-19.
14. A. Alvarez, *Beyond All This Fiddle: Essays 1955-67* (London: The

Penguin Press, 1968), p. 5.

15. Owen Barfield, p. 130.
16. John Bayley, *The Uses of Division: Unity and Disharmony in Literature* (London: Chatto and Windus, 1976), p. 177.
17. Yeats, *A Vision,* p. 8.
18. John Bayley, p. 177.
19. Owen Barfield, p. 147.
20. Arthur C. Danto, *Sartre* (1975; rpt. Glasgow: Fontana, 1982), p. 137.
21. Yeats, *Essays and Introductions,* p. 208.
22. Arthur Danto, p. 138.
23. *Ibid.*
24. Walter Stein, *Criticism as Dialogue* (Cambridge: At the Univ. Press, 1969), pp. 64-65.
25. A. Alvarez, *Beyond All This Fiddle,* p. 15.
26. Stuart Holroyd, *Emergence from Chaos* (Boston: Houghton Mifflin, 1957), p. 117.
27. Yeats, *Autobiographies,* p. 463.
28. *Ibid.,* p. 461.
29. Terence Diggory, *Yeats and American Poetry: The Tradition of the Self* (Princeton: Princeton Univ. Press, 1983), p. 6.
30. *Ibid.,* p. 7.
31. Arthur Danto, p. 41.
32. Owen Barfield, *Worlds Apart: A Dialogue of the 1960's* (London: Faber and Faber, 1963), p. 191.
33. Malcolm Bradbury, "An Age of Parody: Style in the Modern Arts," *Encounter,* Vol. LV, No. I, July 1980, p. 38.
34. Cited from Lionel Trilling's *Sincerity and Authenticity* (1971; rpt. Cambridge: Harvard Univ. Press, 1973), p. 119.
35. Octavio Paz, p. 60.
36. Wallace Stevens, *The Collected Poems of Wallace Stevens* (London: Faber and Faber, 1966), p. 165.
37. Cleanth Brooks, *A Shaping Joy,* p. 108.
38. Cited from *Sincerity and Authenticity,* p. 119.
39. *Essays and Introductions,* p. 254.
40. Frank Lentricchia, *The Gaiety of Language: An Essay on the Radical Poetics of W.B. Yeats and Wallace Stevens* (California: Univ. of California Press, 1968), p. 73.
41. Stuart Holroyd, p. 115.
42. *Selected Criticism and Prose,* p. 266.

43. Yeats, *Autobiographies*, p. 355.
44. Octavio Paz, p. 22.
45. Yeats, *CP*, p. 284.
46. *Selected Criticism and Prose*, p. 170.
47. Cited from Louis MacNeice, "Foreword" to *The Poetry of W.B. Yeats* (1941; rpt. New York: OUP, 1969), p. 10.
48. Yeats, *CP*, p. 240.
49. Henri Bergson, "The Criterion of Individuality: Tragedy Vs Comedy," in *Modern Continental Literary Criticism*, ed. O.B. Hardison, Jr. (New York: Appleton-Century-Crofts, 1962), p. 198.
50. Arthur Danto, p. 36.
51. Cleanth Brooks, *A Shaping Joy*, p. 119.
52. Yeats, *CP*, p. 204.
53. Stuart Holroyd, p. 121.
54. Richard Ellmann, "Robartes and Aherne: Two Sides of a Penny," *The Kenyon Review*, Vol. 10, No. 2, Spring 1948, p. 186.
55. Stuart Holroyd, pp. 130-31.
56. *Ibid.*, p. 120.
57. *Ibid.*, pp. 128-29.
58. Robert Langbaum, *The Mysteries of Identity: A Theme in Modern Literature* (New York: OUP, 1977), p.186.
59. Ernest Wolf, p. 49.
60. Cleanth Brooks, *Modern Poetry and the Tradition*, p. 45.

The Double Vision

Man's nostalgia for a lost paradise and his faint recollection of the vestiges of an existence otherwise obliterated from memory—what Wordsworth refers to as intimations of immortality—relate to a need to regain a sense of rootedness, and to know the "original" truth about himself. In *Troilus and Cressida*, Shakespeare writes:

> The heavens themselves, the planets, and this centre
> Observe degree, priority, and place,
> Insisture, course, proportion, season, form,
> Office, and custom, in all line of order.
> . . . O, when degree is shaked,
> Which is the ladder of all high designs,
> The enterprise is sick. . . .
> Take but degree away, untune that string,
> And hark what discord follows.[1]

The performance of "Dharma" or the observance of Degree is necessary if we are to have a central hold upon life. The search for a centre is not to be dissociated from the desire to unravel the mysteries of identity. They are interrelated as wheel to axle.

Hopkins's "inscape" expressed as:

> Each mortal thing does one thing and the same:
> deals out that being indoors each one dwells;
> Selves—goes itself; myself it speaks and spells,
> crying what I do is me: for that I came[2]

the "swadharma" of the *Bhagavad Gita*, according to which each person must follow the law of his own being, and Yeats's need to be "utterly oneself"—have this in common that they all seek to establish the real centre *within* man.

Despite the modern poet's hopeful declaration:

> The centre that I cannot find
> Is known to my unconscious mind,
> I have no reason to despair
> Because I am already there[3]

and Hopkins's steadfast belief in the uniqueness of each mortal thing, it is difficult to exult in the knowledge of the centred self. It is not surprising that like other poets of his time, though with greater urgency, Yeats sought to grapple with the complexity of the self. It was a problem that intrigued him throughout his life. The quest of the twentieth-century man for identity is the internalization of a primary search for a centre whose axis is located inside himself.

As a process by which man learns to civilize himself, human culture works progressively towards man's self-liberation through art and religion which represent two of the most important efforts by which mankind manifests its impulse to perfect itself. Art and religion share between them the common aspiration for an Ideal world—art, by building a world of its own, and religion, by achieving spiritual unity with a higher domain. In view of the lack of a suitable world to inhabit, the artist's attempt to create another ideal one of his own may be interpreted as an endeavour to keep alive a correspondence between the ideal and the real.

The poet acknowledges man as being multilateral and multi-faced. Yet, he seeks a unity in multiplicity by bringing the contraries in his nature to co-exist in a productive unity. When the self is made the centre, the "still-point of the turning world" cannot be static. Moving on its own axis, it has to be dynamic. In the act of productive unity, like produces like. But the duality, resulting from creative reproduction, remains essentially a unity. Productive Unity by means of a "separative projection," as Coleridge calls it, leads to a polarity which expresses itself once again as unity by its "tendency at once to individuate and connect, to detach but so as either to retain or to reproduce attachment."[4] The polarities may be distinguished from each other, but cannot be separated. By projecting his innermost being into the appearances of nature, the poet unites heart and intellect, self and soul, thought and feeling and, similarly, all opposites. The "condition of such union is passion in the poet—where by passion is understood not mere undetermined feeling, but the deepest stirring of the whole nature, emotion tempered by thought, thought vitalized by emotion."[5] Did not Shakespeare's people make everything serve their passion, a passion wherein the whole energy of their being is momentarily concentrated? Passion which transforms "birds, beasts, men, women, landscape, society" into symbol and metaphor is idea transformed into image because it is charged with emotion and feeling, and there remains "no surface, depth only."[6] We must remember, says Yeats, "that the highest life unites, as in one fire, the greatest passion and the greatest courtesy."[7] Even the artist "who takes up pen or chisel" must not seek originality— "passion is his only business."[8]

As Arthur Mizener says, Yeats accepted reality "only in his own terms, and the main requirement of these terms was that particular version of the romantic objective on which the nineties concentrated: intensity of feeling."[9] In Coleridge, it is "unity of effect, a qualitative resolution expressed in atmosphere and feeling," wherein the imagination "draws intimations of an ultimate unity from immediate severances and divisions not by excluding the difficult forces but by accommodating them."[10] The artist's passion for reality makes the work of art give us "the motions of the human soul in all their depth and variety . . . the dynamic process of life itself—the continuous oscillation between opposite poles."[11] If the artist is able to make harmony out of the chaos of perception it is because "the power of passion itself has been made a formative power."[12]

Unlike the living and generative unity that Coleridge talked about, which pertains to the mind of the poet, the unity which literary critics consider as "value" in modern criticism is closer to "unity-as idea." To transfer the unity that is apprehended by the poet to the poem, the poet must actualize it verbally and imagistically. The symbolic imagination would proceed to embody the apprehended unity through analogy. The imagination as a "coadunating" faculty achieves a balance or equilibrium by bringing the heterogeneous elements together without dissolving their distinctive qualities. By means of symbol, discord is resolved both structurally and phenomenologically. Richards's poetry of inclusion, where all the several effects of the formal elements in a poem are gathered into a single response, becomes honest and true to the nature of human experience when we take into account the productive unity that Coleridge talked about.

A poet who, "in ideal perfection," would bring "the whole soul of man into activity" finds, as he proceeds to embody this unity in art, that he is bound to a medium that does not have all the plasticity he would like it to possess. Just as the reader, on his part, has to overcome several formal veils to make the transition from the semantic level to the soul of the poet, the poet has to battle with many inherent limitations of his medium before he can give a convincing evidence of the unity of which he has an intuitive apprehension. He knows that language is a limited medium, yet he is condemned to make meaning only through it—language being the visible embodiment of the nature of the poet's mind.

Apart from being a committed craftsman, Yeats was also profoundly concerned about the problem of Man and his relation to the world. Therefore, the limitations of the "medium" posed a special kind of dilemma to him. He knew that reconciliation is not possible without dialectical opposition. He saw "consciousness as conflict." But, with conflict, there would never be final reconciliation. This contradictory nature of conflict—with it, the unity would always threaten to break into diversity, and without it, there would be no life, no consciousness—was exploited by Yeats to achieve his kind of poetic integration.

Unity of being as a generative principle, productive in terms of sameness and difference, is not possible to realize in a medium which, without the presence of conflict, is by itself incapable of a suggestion of dynamic unity or balanced tension. Yeats solved the problem on the formal level by making use of masks, often creating two opposite characters or voices, as in *Ego Dominus Tuus* and *A Dialogue of Self and Soul.* In "Poetry and Tradition" Yeats said that "the nobleness of the arts is in the mingling of contraries."[13] What we look for in art is a dialectical unity—the kind we find in the best of Yeats's later poetry—wherein the self conducts an "interior monologue" with its direct opposite, the anti-self.

The masks serve another purpose as well. They fulfil the need to be "utterly oneself." They suggest the multiplicity and contradictions inherent in the self without overshadowing the power of a single, lyrical voice. The mask could perform the aesthetic function of prolonging conflict in order to make the final unity more meaningful, and also reveal aspects of the poet's personality. To sustain the mask at the psychological level, Yeats adopted conflict as his idiom. Conflict would generate further conflict, making it possible for the poet to achieve, even in a momentary unity, a living polarity.

In *Vacillation* Yeats writes that even as "man runs his course" "between extremities," a "brand, or flaming breath,/ Comes to destroy/ All those antinomies." And,

> While on the shop and street I gazed
> My body of a sudden blazed;
> And twenty minutes more or less
> It seemed, so great my happiness,
> That I was blessed and could bless.

These indefinable experiences of harmony are rare. They occur only at peak moments in one's life when all that in harsh and discordant in one's self dissolves into a sweet, exultant blessed mood.

Though it seemed that he had found what he wanted, Yeats wrote in one of his last letters, "Man can embody truth but he cannot know it."[14] The wish to embody it, at the completion of his life was always there. And yet, for some reason, it was constantly evaded. A reconciliation involving the necessity of a single choice was something he had, perhaps, never anticipated. He would have found it difficult to accept integration by exclusion. Moreover, his experience had been such that whenever he rejected some part of life, a new experience made him receive it once again, forcing him to resign to the fact that what he had rejected formed an essential part of the whole. For example, though he supported Irish freedom, he disliked the violent approach of some of the revolutionaries. The Easter Rising of 1916 changed it all. He had to accept, if not the worth, at least the fact of their sacrifice. Similarly, again, his indignation against the shopkeeping morality of the Dublin folk had made him believe that Romantic Ireland was dead and gone. Yet, when he wrote his Will, he committed himself to the common folk of Ireland. If he owed a poetic debt, it was not to the high and the noble but, as he acknowledged, to

> A mound of refuse or the sweepings of a street,
> Old kettles, old bottles, and a broken can,
> Old iron, old bones, old rags, that raving slut
> Who keeps the till.

Whatever he tried to set aside was thrown into his path, and what he cherished most was denied to him. He admired active men but could not himself be one. He had the advice of his father who said that "in a rich and abundant nature a single feeling in time takes to itself other feelings, and the poet of many feelings resumes the sovereign power, and the man of action departs however reluctantly."[15] But Yeats may have seen that this was a poetic solution to a practical problem and, therefore, doubted the possibility of a final statement. He could not have deliberately avoided it. It was not an unwillingness to make the choice but the complexity of making one that was felt and demonstrated. There may have been an impulse to resolve the tension, an impulse from within to decide, once and for all, between dream and action. But he perhaps saw that, as in the case of the Irish airman, though the fullness achieved in the moment of resolution was life at its zenith where the tensions were totally dissolved, it was a fullness of life for which the price was also life itself. It turned out to be too expensive. If the poet was not prepared to pay that price, it was because, in that exhilarating moment of complete fulfilment, he saw the terrible face of death. Out of ecstatic joy came tragic realization. Each time he protested, he grew in self-knowledge. Perhaps it also brought him a certain peace. He wrote to Ethel Mannin that he found his peace by pitting his sole nature against something and the greater the tension, the greater the self-knowledge.

Though there is no critical unanimity with regard to Yeats's poetry, no matter what seemingly controversial methods he used, Yeats managed to create, out of the incongruous material of life at his disposal, an artistic triumph. The masks were, in view of the greater purpose of exhausing life's possibilities, not merely rhetorical strategy. Behind them were the deep convictions of a man whose mind has ceased to judge or to reason because he has seen that everything is inextricably linked up with its opposite. It is true that among "subjective men . . . the victory is an intellectual daily re-creation of all that exterior fate snatches away, and so that fate's antithesis; while what I have called 'the Mask' is an emotional antithesis to all that comes out of their internal nature."[16] The preservation of the integrity of the self was more important than "mental consistency." His father had told him:

> A poet should feel quite free to say in the morning that he believes in marriage and in the evening that he now no longer believes in it; in the morning that he believes in God and in the evening that he does not believe in God, the important thing being not that he keep his mental consistency but that he preserve the integrity of his soul.[17]

What Yeats wrote about art in general is true of his own art when the "struggle for complete affirmation" becomes his art's "chief poignancy." Eliot aptly pointed out that though Yeats was born "in a world in which the doctrine of 'Art for Art's sake' was generally accepted," and lived on into one in which art began to acquire public importance and demanded social relevance, "he held firmly to the right view which is between these" and "showed that an artist, by serving his art with entire integrity, is at the same time rendering the greatest service he can to his own nation and to the whole world."[18] If we look under the superficial experiences of the characters created by the poet, we find a sensitive nature struggling to be free and raising, in the process of aspiring for the impossible, the important question of whether it is possible at all to be truly oneself. The nature of the questions he asked and sought to answer ought to justify the adoption of contrary norms that rebuke accepted conventions. The daring attempts to fathom the depths of the abyss of the self were aimed at defying the limitations of human life. No effort to get closer to the truth seemed wasted or unnecessary. As soon as a particular instrument had served its purpose, it was discarded for something better—as if "every imaginative construct could only momentarilly satisfy his creative need and must then be demolished."[19]

The mask and the technique of "dialogue," seen from this broader perspective, serve a dual function. They uphold the changing appearances of life by engendering fresh conflicts, and also act as a heuristic strategy, taking the reader—through a labyrinthine search—closer to the heart of the poem. Yeats does appear, occasionally, to set aside the mask and speak in his own voice. It seems as if a poem in which the "I" gives an account of responses to a particular event or person is the poet speaking, at last, in his real voice. Deceptively, an incident from private life is taken, or a friend mentioned, to give the impression of an apparently personal revelation. To deliberately mislead the reader, an artist may create an illusion and then dispel it. He may fabricate himself to render an ostentatiously personal utterance, and may be truly himself behind an artificial construction. In "First Principles," Yeats says that if the artist's work "does not seem, when it comes, to be the creation of a new personality, in a few years it will not seem to be alive at all."[20]

It is evident that the unconventionality and complexity of modern poetry calls for a new mode of criticism and approach. Like the Indian metaphysician who says that Brahman can only be described in terms of what He is not (neti, neti, i.e., "not this, not this"), the essential meanings of modern poetry may be brought out only in terms of what an individual poem avoids saying rather than what it does state, that is, the "real" text may be apprehended as present by its being noticeably absent. A poem is to be explained by the elements which arc conspicuous by their absence. Yeats, borrowing the psychological aspect of this idea from Jung, said that we can complete the self only by focussing on its opposite, the anti-self. The contention that the older Yeats lacked a spiritual or, at least, a philosophical bent of mind whose absence is discernible in his later poetry, may be refuted on the ground that the excessive preoccupation with the body or decrepit age or the loss of vigour was a defensive measure adopted by the poetic self to make meaning in terms of an awareness not so much of a "presence" as of the "absence" of an element. By being made conspicuous by its absence, what is not stated becomes, in practice, the central focus of the poem.

In *Sailing to Byzantium,* Yeats crowds the first stanza with imagery of life and generation which belongs to "that country" which is not for old men. When actually crowding the stanza with emotions that are contrary to what he proposed to deal with, he is not inadvertently suggesting the impossibility of rejecting "sensual music." Instead, Yeats is drawing attention to the dire necessity of shaking off its powerful spell—its power is concretized in the images he uses in the stanza—especially at a time when the body to which the sick-with-desire heart is fastened has become a "dying animal." While entangled in life's meshes, one is "caught," as it were, in its sensual music against one's will, in a kind of spell. Drawn into its influence, one neglects "monuments of unaging intellect."

There is a reluctance, no doubt, to make the change, particularly when it involves exchanging vibrant life for deathless but lifeless monuments. A poet knows that if he is to continue writing poetry, a poetry that endures, it has to be a poetry of strength, born of combat. To contrive a combat—all art being a contrivance—would be easy if the combative elements were the same as those that were the cause of the deep and perplexing conflict of his life—namely, life and art, body and intellect, self and soul. To reconcile to the philosophical could not have been quite as difficult as it is made out to be. But, eventually, such reconciliation would have done irreparable harm to the poetic instinct. This is why a final resolution was perhaps always postponed and even deliberately thrust aside. The image of the "comfortable kind of old scarecrow" and "sixty-year-old smiling public man" might have lured him—as at one time it was a woman's face or worse—from the craft of verse, the "accustomed toil." But the easy solution had nothing heroic about it. And he would still be one of the "indomitable Irishry."

"Supreme art," said Yeats, "is a traditional statement of certain heroic and religious truths, passed on from age to age, modified by individual genius, but never abandoned."[21] His individual genius sought to bring the several concerns—Irish folklore, Irish politics, theosophy—into poetry, holding them together in a "single thought" so that the "mythology, the politics, and the magic are conceived, through the personalities that reflected them, with an increasing unity of apprehension."[22]

Though Yeats and Eliot apparently differed in their poetic practice, what they tried to achieve is nearly the same. Both of them were interested in the self. While Yeats, in his obsessive concern about the making of the self, was constantly engaged in finding ways and means of going nearer to that ideal in terms of its opposite, Eliot, professing impersonality, still had his eye on the self he was moving away from. The "multiple selves" of Yeats come close to the "impersonality" of Eliot when, in effect, they become equally impersonal. The poet who, expressing the desire to shore the fragmented self against the ruins of a broken culture, said: "Shall I at least set my lands in order?,"[23] could not have possessed a very different outlook from the one who said: "Myself must I remake."[24] The difference is that Yeats discovered his poetic "swadharma" by pursuing the path of the symbolic artist. He did not lack, as Eliot did, the "dimension of human error."[25] Perhaps, as Alvarez puts it, Yeats's strength lies in his honest acceptance of human fallibility. He did not make the mistake that an "angelic imagination" like

Poe's made. By overleaping and cheating the human condition, the angelic intellect, seeing nothing, condemns itself to silence.

It is presumption on the part of man to think that he can know essence directly. By circumventing the natural world and placing himself in the "seat of God," as Tate says, the angelic imagination exhausts intellectual force because it lacks any real "object." It is not possible for the human intellect to reach God as essence, "only God as analogy," i.e., by analogy to the natural world. Unity-as being may be apprehended potentially by an intuitive understanding but can be actualized only in terms of unity-as idea. Unity-as idea can be re-converted into unity-as being in the duration of the experience of the poem, in the encounter or meeting of a sensitive reader and the persona of the poem. The poet and reader have to meet in the "experiencing persona," each conferring value on the other. But unity-as idea has to invariably resort to "image" or to "symbol"—in other words, it must take refuge in analogy.

If Dante had the vision of God or essence, Tate explains, it was because his Triune Circle was light, apprehendable by the finite intellect and senses. Poe, on the other hand, made his centre "where the sun is silent." By refusing to relate to nature, he condemned himself to seeing nothing. In the words of Tate:

> The reach of our imaginative enlargement is perhaps no longer than the ladder of analogy, at the top of which we may see all, if we still wish to see anything, that we have brought up with us from the bottom, where lies the sensible world. If we take nothing with us to the top but our emptied, angelic intellects, we shall see nothing when we get there.[26]

Yeats's *Circus Animals' Desertion* wherein the poet enumerates the "masterful images" which "grew in pure mind" is a "ladder" that the poet has climbed by means of analogy to the utterly human situation. The symbolic poet may begin with unpurged images—"a mound of refuse or the sweepings of a street"—but when these pass through the "purer mind," in tranquil restoration, they give rise to masterful images.

Like Coleridge, Poe exalts the imagination but in an entirely different way. The cartesian vacuum of the angelic imagination pretends that the "threshold" between poetic intellect and knowledge of essence does not exist. The two extreme standpoints are that either one denies that the "threshold" is a threshold, leading to subjective idealism, or, as Barfield points out, one fortifies and strengthens the barrier between the two worlds in a way that would make it impassable.[27]

Drawing our attention to the opening scene of the *Bhagavad Gita* wherein, standing in the midst of the two armies before the commencement of battle, Arjuna suddenly finds in himself no desire to fight, Barfield makes an interesting statement. Krishna's endeavour to transpose the warrior-prince's thinking to a new dimension and realm where all the objections Arjuna has raised against the killing of his kith and kin become unreal, and yet his exhortation to Arjuna to "fight on" would be intelligible, Barfield says, if we recognize the inner implications of this apparent contradiction. In that other dimension different rules apply, and we are not to draw conclusions for the lower plane from what derives at the higher one. The ordinary logical categories of the lower plane do not hold there. Moreover, simply because what we do in our plane becomes unimportant from the point of view of the higher plane does not mean that we are to stop doing or acting according to the natural character of the plane to which we belong. We are to follow the laws of the lower plane, not overstep them unnaturally. The *Gita* does not imply that the threshold between the two planes of consciousness cannot be crossed. What it obviously means is that "though it may be crossed, it does not cease for that reason to exist." In other words, it cannot be left unaccounted for.

Krishna's argument further expanded would mean that simply because you know the appearances of nature to be unreal does not permit and justify your acting false to the "dharma" laid down specifically for your fulfilment. However imperfect and limited your own "dharma" may be in comparison with another's, you are not for that reason to give up your own. Dire consequences would result from trying to go against one's own natural aptitude. The poet's apprehension of essence that belongs to a non-human realm must also be through the observance of the rules of the consciousness to which be belongs. Correspondingly, Yeats's achievement of a unity that disregards the "pull of the dark moon and the full" would be a betrayal of his personal and poetic identity. It would belie his own nature and self. He cannot cheat the human that has nurtured the poetic self. To do so would be to pretend to directly intuit essence. If the poetic intellect must know the truth, it must be by analogy to some concrete form or other. The poet cannot overstep the natural limitations that belong to his craft and situation in life. He must discover his identity through his own poetic "swadharma." Otherwise, when he reaches the top, he will see nothing. The image or symbol he creates has to be of the phenomenal world even when it refers to the noumenal.

We may recall that when Krishna invites Arjuna to cross the threshold into a higher realm by showing him a vision of the reality of that realm, Arjuna is terrified. His terror is equivalent to our own, however disguised ours may be, when we use emotional overtones to reject "occult qualities" from scientific enquiry. It partly explains why we call Yeats's interest in the occult and oriental wisdom "dabbling." In his earnestness to resolve, once and for all, the problem of the "threshold," Yeats often resorted to very unconventional methods. His anxiety to arrive at a solution grew with age, never deserted him. As a symbolic poet, he did not wish to leap the human, as the angelic intellect does, to get to the world of essence. "What matter if the ditches are impure?," he said in *A Dialogue of Self and Soul.* He is content. He will climb to the top on the ladder of analogy. The "dharma" of the angelic intellect is not for him. He will remain faithful to the role of the symbolic poet, untempted by the promise of a direct intuition of essence. Yeats achieved poetic integration drawing together all the levels into a unity of experience. He preferred to see the face of truth via poetry, however bitter the final experience might prove to be.

The fundamental outlook of the West often amounts to a denial of the threshold as a threshold. If natural science made it the boundary between existence and nothingness, it was still a boundary, a terminus, not a threshold. The materialistic and positivistic philosophy of the century gave no complementary answer. After Freud and Jung it was not possible to believe that what lay beyond one's plane was unknowable. How could truth remain out of reach when the unconscious was a storehouse of all knowledge? Yeats wanted to explore the treasury of the unconscious because he thought he would find there knowledge which would unravel the mysteries of identity. True, he did not use the word "threshold" or refer to it as such, but his interest in the Occult suggests that the problem did intermittently, if not persistently, disturb him. Yeats had pledged his allegiance to Man, to "upstanding men," and if he had to work out his poetic liberation, it had to be through analogy to the human. His early dream to go beyond the world of pain and sorrow to an Ideal world of Everlasting Joy was perhaps a reflection of an unvoiced need to cross the threshold.

Ever since genius began to be understood as something that lay within the man of genius so that he is no longer possessed by it but possesses it, the concept of the Imagination as a faculty which can facilitate a transition from one realm to another, has been gaining importance. The Imagination has been recognized as the "most indispensable factor in the products of works of art, and particularly perhaps, of poetry."[28] The poet accepts the presence of a threshold, in fact, works with it and uses it. But his task is to relate, through the Imagination, both sides of the threshold. The Coleridgean idea of Unity that breaks into duality only to come together again in a new combination is one wherein a reconciliation of opposites is achieved without trying to dissolve the individual identity of either. The mind "can be rendered intuitive of the spiritual in man" but for this it needs a mediator. The Imagination as a shaping and modifying power is uniquely suited to perform this role. It can help the mind to cross from one plane to another by working through analogy. It can also make the transition smooth, taking care to see that the distinctions are not blurred completely. The distinctive individualities may be maintained even while a tensional unity or balance is sustained. If the two sides are tasted as single—as though the threshold does not exist—it would result in what may be called "confusion of Babel"—a mistake of exercising and applying the laws and categories of one side to another. Moreover, to treat the two as single would be to think of a unity without multiplicity. When a poet enters the heart of such "original" unity he surrenders to silence because it is a unity which is too fundamental to be conceived of. A poet cannot afford to barter his creative power for "impotent silence." He must have the WORD. And, having the Word means that he must also terminate every effort of his in the creation of an Image.

Yeats acknowledged the presence of two planes or levels of consciousness. But he did not want Unity by cancelling any one out. The attempt was rather in favour of keeping the two realms in a balanced tension. With the masks he could speak now from one pole of his being and now from another, and achieve, as Bayley says, "negative capability by numbers." By speaking from two poles at the same time, he could engender conflict as well. When we say that conflict led to fresh conflicts, prolonging the creative act and the life of the poetic instinct, enabling him to enact the "daily victory of the Image, what we are suggesting is that given the premise of a threshold to be crossed the unity which Yeats achieved was the only kind he could have achieved. It is the only meaningful kind of unity a poet *can* achieve—a Unity wherein the opposites are held separate and yet united in a tension of polarity, each predominating in alternation. It is a unity achieved in terms of dipolarity or the double vision of Blake.

In rejecting a strict adherence to the French Symbolist practice, Yeats demonstrated his own attitude to art. The French Symbolist removed himself as far from Man as possible. His was an artistic accomplishment but in that world man had no place. An artist who cheats Man places himself at the heights where only the Gods live. Yeats wanted no part in this kind of achievement. Even the "Gods who possess the heavens, covet the earth." He would explore the infinite possibilities of Becoming before entering the realm of Being.

To climb the ladder could not have been difficult, given his determination, intense passion and the powerful imaginative capability. But, to come down from the top needed an extraordinary amount of courage. If Yeats showed himself willing to take the risk it was perhaps because he saw no meaning in climbing to the top if it did not embrace the erroneous being that man is. To reach the top without resorting to analogy would be to pretend one did not share in the human condition. On the other hand, to use a ladder would mean not only that one had to start from the bottom, but also that when one was at the topmost rung, the ladder would still touch the ground. To reject the ladder once one had reached the top would be equivalent to kicking against the life that had sustained him. Without the ladder of analogy, the possibility of return to the sensible world to enact another victory in the creation of a unified image would be closed to the poet. It would mean death of the poetic instinct. Yeats chose to remain a poet. There was this consolation, however, that life would not betray him if he could refuse to "lie down where all the ladders start." Life would beget fresh images. Returning to the foul rag-and-bone shop of the heart, he could each time ascend anew. This cyclical process could go on endlessly and he could remain a poet in defiance of life's limitations.

Beginning with productive unity, the polarities are made to extend all over its length, converging and diverging into new unities like the centripetal and centrifugal forces, never losing sight of the centre.

How can we cast a cold eye on such a poetic achievement? We must know that "when all words are said," and

> a man is fighting mad,
> Something drops from eyes long blind,
>   He completes his partial mind,
> For an instant stands at ease,
>   Laughs aloud, his heart at peace.[29]

NOTES

1. Shakespeare, *Complete Works*, I, iii, 85-111.
2. *The Poems of Gerald Manley Hopkins*, p. 90.
3. W.H. Auden, *The Collected Poetry of W.H. Auden* (New York: Random House, 1945), p. 10.
4. Cited from *Romanticism Comes of Age*, p. 157.
5. Shawcross ed., *Biographia Literaria*, p. xxxiv.
6. Yeats, *Autobiographies*, pp. 291-92.
7. *Selected Criticism and Prose*, p. 148.
8. *Ibid.*, p. 177.
9. From *W.B. Yeats: A Critical Anthology*, p. 178.
10. Denis Donoghue, *The Sovereign Ghost*, p. 18.
11. Cassirer, *An Essay on Man*, p. 148.
12. *Ibid.*
13. *Selected Criticism and Prose*, p. 164.
14. *W.B. Yeats: A Critical Anthology*, p. 136.
15. *Ibid.*, p. 66.
16. Yeats, *Autobiographies*, p. 189.
17. Cited from Richard Ellmann's *Man and the Masks*, p. 19.
18. *Selected Prose*, p. 205.
19. *Modern Poetry: Essays in Criticism*, ed. John Hollander, p. 406.
20. *Selected Criticism and Prose*, p. 139.
21. Yeats, *Autobiographies*, p. 490.
22. *W.B. Yeats: A Critical Anthology*, p. 128.
23. Edward Leeson, p. 441.
24. *CP*, p. 347.
25. A. Alvarez, *The Shaping Spirit*, p. 32.
26. Allen Tate, *The Man of Letters*, p. 131. By "angelic imagination" Tate means the apprehension of essence without analogy to the human symbol. It involves the Will and Intellect as against Imagination and Emotion. Tate prefers the symbolic imagination, whose exemplars are Dante, Yeats and others.
27. Owen Barfield, "Imagination and Inspiration," *Interpretation: The Poetry of Meaning*, pp. 61-63.
28. *Ibid.*, p. 65.
29. Yeats, *CP*, p. 398.

BIBLIOGRAPHY

I. Works

Autobiographies. 1955; rpt. London: Papermac, 1980.

The Collected Poems of W.B. Yeats. 2nd ed., 1933; rpt. London: Papermac, 1982.

Eleven Plays of William Butler Yeats. Ed. A.Norman Jeffares. New York: Collier Books; 1964.

Essays and Introductions. 1961; rpt. London: Macmillan, 1971.

Letters on Poetry by W.B. Yeats to Dorothy Wellesley. Introduction by Kathleen Raine. 1940; rpt. London: Oxford University Press, 1964.

Mythologies. New York: Collier Books, 1969.

Running to Paradise. An Introductory selection by Kevin Crossley--Holland. London: Macmillan, 1967.

Selected Criticism and Prose. Ed. A. Norman Jeffares. 1964; London: Pan Books in association with Macmillan London, 1980.

Selected Poems and Two Plays of William Butler Yeats. Ed. M.L. Rosenthal. 1903; New York: Collier Books, 1962.

Uncollected Prose, Vol. I. First Reviews and artcles (1886 to 1896) collected and edited by John P. Frayne. London: Macmillan, 1970.

Uncollected Prose, Vol. II. Reviews, articles and other miscellaneous prose (1897 to 1939). Collected and edited by John P. Frayne and Colton Johnson. London: Macmillan, 1975.

A Vision. 1937; London: Papermac, 1981.

II Critical Studies

Adams, Hazard. "Yeatsian Art and Mathematic Form." *The Centennial Review*, Vol. IV, No. 1, Winter, 1960.

Albright, Daniel. *The Myth Against Myth: A Study of Yeats's Imagination in Old Age*. London: OUP, 1972.

Allen, James Lovic. "Unity of Archetypes, Myth and Religious Imagery in the Work of Yeats." *Twentieth-Century Literature*, Vol. 20, No. 2, April 1974, pp. 91-95.

Allen, James L. "Yeats's Bird-Soul Symbolism." *Twentieth-Century Literature*, Vol. 6, No. 3, October 1960, pp. 117-22.

Alvarez, A. *Beyond All This Fiddle: Essays 1955-1967*. London: The Penguin Press, 1968.

------. *The Shaping Spirit: Studies in Modern English and American Poets*. London: Chatto and Windus, 1958.

Armstrong, Robert. *The Poetic Vision: Signposts and Landmarks in Poetry*.

London: The Mitre Press, 1973.

Auden, W.H. "Yeats as an Example." *The Kenyon Review*, Vol. X, No. 2, Spring 1948, pp. 187-95.

Bayley, John, *The Romantic Survival: A Study in Poetic Evolution*. London: Constable, 1957.

------. *The Uses of Division: Unity and Disharmony in Literature*. London: Chatto and Windus, 1976.

Bentley, Eric. "Yeats as a Play-Wright." *The Kenyon Review*, Vol. 10, No. 2, Spring 1948, pp. 196-208.

Bhargava, Ashok. *The Poetry of W.B. Yeats: Myth as Metaphor*. New Delhi: Arnold Heinemann, 1979.

Balckmur, R.P. *Form and Value in Modern Poetry*. New York: Doubleday Anchor Books, 1957.

Bloom, Harold. *Yeats*. 1970; rpt. London: OUP, 1972.

Bohlmann, Otto. *Yeats and Nietzsche: An Exploration of Major Nietzschean Echoes in the Writings of William Butler Yeats*. The Macmillan Press, 1982.

Bornstein, George. *Yeats and Shelley*. Chicago: Univ. of Chicago Press, 1970.

Bowra, C.M. *The Heritage of Symbolism*. 1943; rpt. London: Macmillan, 1973.

Bradford, Curtis B. "George Yeats: Poet's Wife." *The Sewanee Review*, Vol. 77, No. 3, Summer 1969, pp. 385-404.

Brooke, Nicholas. "Crazy Jane and 'Byzantium'." *Essays and Studies*. 27 (1974), pp. 68-83.

Brooks, Cleanth. *The Hidden God: Studies in Hemingway, Faulkner, Yeats, Eliot, and Warren*. 1963; rpt. New Haven: Yale University Press, 1969.

Brown, Forman G. "Mr. Yeats and the Supernatural." *The Sewanee Review*, Vol. 33, 1925, pp. 323-34.

Bushrui, Suheil. "Yeats: The Poet as Hero." *Essays and Studies*, 1982, pp. 101-23.

Clarke, Austin. "The Cardinal and the Countess." *Ariel*, Vol. 3, No. 3, July 1972, pp. 58-65.

Critics of Yeats: Readings in Literary Criticism. Ed. Raymond Cowell. London: George Allen and Unwin, 1971.

Diggory, Terence. *Yeats and American Poetry: The Tradition of the Self*. Princeton: Princeton Univ. Press, 1983.

Donoghue, Denis. *The Ordinary Universe: Soundings in Modern Literature*. London: Faber and Faber, 1968.

------. "Tradition, Poetry and W.B. Yeats." *The Sewanee Review*, Vol. 69, No. 3, Summer 1961, pp. 476-84.

------. "The Vigour of its Blood: Yeats's 'Works for Music Perhaps'." *The Kenyon Review*, Vol. 21, No. 3, Summer 1959, pp. 376-87.

------. *Yeats*. 1971; rpt. Glasgow: Fontana, 1982.

Earnshaw, H.G. *Modern Writers: A Guide to Twentieth Century Literature in the English Language*. Edinburgh/London: W. and R. Chambers, 1968.

Elliot, Maurice. "Yeats and the Professors." *Ariel*, Vol. 3, No. 3, July 1972, pp. 5-30.

Ellis, Stephen Paul. "Yeats and Dante." *Comparative Literature*, Vol. 33, No. 1, Winter 1981, pp. 1-17.

Ellmann, Richard. "The Art of Yeats: Affirmative Capability." *The Kenyon Review*, Vol. 15, No. 3. Summer 1953, pp. 357-85.

------. "Black Magic Against White: Aleister Crowley versus W.B. Yeats." *Partisan Review*, Vol. 15, No. 9, September, 1948, pp. 1049-51.

------. *Eminent Domain: Yeats Among Wilde, Joyce, Pound, Eliot and Auden*. New York: OUP, 1967.

------. *The Identity of Yeats*. London: Macmillan, 1954.

------. "Joyce and Yeats." *The Kenyon Review*, Vol. XII, No. 4, Autumn 1950, pp. 618-38.

------. "Robartes and Aherne: Two Sides of a Penny." *The Kenyon Review*, Vol. 10, No. 2, Spring 1948, pp. 177-86.

------. *Yeats: The Man and the Masks*. 1949; rpt. London: Faber and Faber, 1969.

------. "Yeats Without Analogue." *The Kenyon Review*, Vol. 26, No. 1, Winter 1964, pp. 30-47.

------. "Yeats Without Panoply." *The Sewanee Review*, Vol. 64, No. 1, Winter 1956, pp. 145-51.

Feder, Lillian. *Ancient Myth in Modern Poetry*. Princeton: Princeton University Press, 1971.

Fraser, G.S. *The Modern Writer and His World*. 1953; rev. London: Andre Deutsch, 1964.

Frazier, Adrian. "The Ascendancy Poetry of W.B. Yeats." *The Sewanee Review*, Vol. 88, No. 1, Winter 1980, pp. 67-85.

Fullwood, Daphne. "The Early Poetry of W.B. Yeats." *Ariel*, Vol. 3, No. 3, July 1972, pp. 80-90.

Gordon, D.J. *W.B. Yeats: Images of a Poet*. With Contributions by Ian Fletcher, Frank Kermode and Robin Skelton. 1961; rpt. Connecticut: Greenwood Press, 1979.

Grubb, H.T. Hunt. "William Butler Yeats: His Plays, Poems and Sources of Inspiration." *The Poetry Review*, Vol. 26, 1935 (Kraus rpt. 1969), pp. 351-66 and 445-65.

Guthrie, William Norman. "Two Poets: I W.B. Yeats." *The Sewanee Review*, Vol. 9, 1901; rpt. New York: Kraus, 1963, pp. 328-31.

Haeusermann, H.V. "W.B. Yeats's Criticism of Ezra Pound." *The Sewanee Review*, Vol. 57, No. 3, Summer 1949, pp. 437-55.

Hamburger, Michael. *The Truth of Poetry: Tensions in Modern Poetry from Baudelaire to the 1960s*. Manchester: Carcanet New Press, 1969.

Hanagan, Thomas. "Yeats, Joyce and the Matter of Ireland." *Critical Inquiry*, Vol. 2, No. 1, Autumn 1975, pp. 43-67.

Harper, George Mills. *W.B. Yeats and W.T. Horton: The Record of an Occult Friendship*. London: Macmillan, 1980.

------. *Yeats's Golden Dawn*. London: Macmillan, 1974.

Harrison, John R. *The Reactionaries*. London: Victor Gollancz, 1967.

Haydn, Hisam. "The Last of the Romantics: An Introduction to the Symbolism of William Butler Yeats." *The Sewanee Review*, Vol. 55, 1947, pp. 297-323.

Healy, J.V. "Yeats and His Imagination." *The Sewanee Review*, Vol. 54, 1946, pp. 650-59.

Henn, T.R. *The Lonely Tower: Studies in the Poetry of W.B. Yeats*. 2nd ed. 1950; rev. London: Methuen, 1965.

Hodges, Robert R. "The Irony of Yeats's 'Long-Legged Fly'." *Twentieth-Century Literature*, Vol. 12, No. 1, April 1966, pp. 27-30.

Hoffmann, Daniel. *Barbarous Knowledge: Myth in the Poetry of Yeats, Graves, and Muir*. 1967; London: OUP, 1970.

Holbrook, David. *Lost Bearings in English Poetry*. London: Vision Press, 1977.

Holroyd, Stuart. *Emergence from Chaos*. Boston: Houghton Mifflin, 1957.

Hough, Graham. *The Last Romantics*. 1949; rpt. London: Gerald Duckworth, 1961.

------. *Selected Essays*. 1978; rpt. Cambridge: Cambridge University Press, 1980.

Huxley, D.J. "Yeats and Dr. Gogarty." *Ariel*, Vol. 3, No. 3, July 1972, pp. 31-47.

Hynes, Samuel. "All the Wild Witches: The Woman in Yeats's Poems." *The Sewanee Review*, Vol. 85, No. 4, Fall 1977, pp. 565-82.

------. *The Auden Generation: Literature and Politics in England in the 1930s*. London: The Bodley Head, 1976.

In Excited Reverie: A Centenary Tribute to William Butler Yeats--1865-1939. Ed. A. Norman Jeffares and K.G.W. Cross. London: Macmillan, 1965.

Islam, Shamsul. "The Influence of Eastern Philosophy on Yeats's Later Poetry." *Twentieth-Century Literature*, Vol. 19, No. 4, Oct 1973, pp. 283-90.

Jain, Sushil Kumar. "Indian Elements in the Poetry of Yeats: On Chatterjee and Tagore." *Comparative Literature*, Vol. 7, No. 1, March 1970, pp. 82-96.

Jeffares, A. Norman. *The Circus Animals: Essays on W.B. Yeats*. London: Macmillan, 1970

------. *A Commentary on the Collected Poems of W.B. Yeats*. 1968; rpt. London: Macmillan, 1971.

------. *The Poetry of W.B. Yeats*. 1961; rpt. London: Edward Arnold, 1964.

------. *W.B. Yeats. The Profiles in Literature Series*. London: Routledge and Kegan Paul, 1971.

------. *W.B. Yeats: Man and Poet*. London: Routledge and Kegan Paul, 1962.

Kermode, Frank. *Romantic Image*. 1957; rpt. London: Routledge and Kegan Paul, 1966.

Koch, Vivienne. *W.B. Yeats: The Tragic Phase: A Study of the Last Poems*. London: Routledge and Kegan Paul, 1951.

Langbaum, Robert. "The Exteriority of Self in Yeats's Poetry and Thought." *NLH*, Vol VII, No. 3, Spring 1976, pp. 579-97.

------. *The Mysteries of Identity: A Theme in Modern Literature*. New York: OUP, 1977.

Leavis, F.R. *New Bearings in English Poetry: A Study of the Contemporary Situation*. 1932; rpt. London: Chatto and Windus, 1959.

Lentricchia, Frank. *The Gaiety of Language: The Essay on the Radical Poetics of W.B. Yeats and Wallace Stevens*. California: University of California Press, 1968.

Letters to W.B. Yeats. Ed. Richard J. Finneran and George Mills Harper and William M. Murphy, Vol. I and II. London: Macmillan Press, 1977.

Lynch, David. *Yeats: The Poetic of the Self*. Chicago: The University of Chicago Press, 1979.

MacLiammoir, Michael, et al. *W.B. Yeats and His World*. London: Thames and Hudson, 1971.

MacNeice, Louis. *The Poetry of W.B. Yeats*. 1941; rpt. New York: OUP, 1969.

Malins, Edward. *A Preface to Yeats*. 1974; rpt. Essex: Longman, 1983.

Martin, Augustine, "'The Secret Rose' and Yeats's Dialogue with History." *Ariel*, Vol. 3, No. 3, July 1972, pp. 91-103.

Martin, Graham. "Fine Manners, Liberal Speech: A Note on the Public Poetry of W.B. Yeats." *Essays in Criticism*, Vol. 2, 1961 (1966 rpt).

Melchiori, Giorgio. *The Whole Mystery of Art: Pattern into Poetry in the Work of W.B. Yeats*. London: Routledge and Kegan Paul, 1960.

Menon, V.K.Narayana. *The Development of William Butler Yeats*. 1942; rev. London: Oliver and Boyd, 1960.

Merivale, Patricia. "'Ultima Thule': Ghosts and Borderlines in Yeats and Rilke." *Comparative Literature*, Vol. 30, No. 3, Summer 1978, pp. 249-67.

Mikhail, E.H., ed. *W.B. Yeats: Interviews and Recollections*, Vol. I. London: The Macmillan Press, 1977.

------. *W.B. Yeats: Interviews and Recollections*, Vol. II. London: The Macmillan Press, 1977.

Miller, J. Hillis. *Poets of Reality: Six Twentieth Century Writers*. Massachusetts: The Belknap Press of Harvard University Press, and London: OUP, 1966.

Milne, Fred L. "Yeats's 'The Cap and Bells': A Probable Indebtedness to Tennyson's 'Maud'." *Ariel*, Vol. 3, No. 3, July 1972, pp. 69-79.

Modern Poetry: Essays in Criticism. Ed. John Hollander. London: OUP, 1968.

Moore, John Rees. "The Janus Face: Yeats's Player Queen." *The Sewanee Review*, Vol. 76, No. 4, Autumn 1968, pp. 608-30.

Moore, Richard. "The Balancer: Yeats and His Supernatural System." *The Yale Review*, 72, No. 3, April, 1983, pp. 385-98.

Murphy, William M. "Father and Son: The Early Education of William Butler Yeats." *A Review of English Literature*, Vol. VII, No. 4, October, 1967, pp. 75-96.

Olney, James. "Father and Son: J.B. Yeats and W.B. Yeats." *The South Atlantic Quarterly*, 79, No. 3, Summer 1980, pp. 321-28.

------. "W.B. Yeats's Diamonic Memory." *The Sewanee Review*, Vol. 85, No. 4, Fall 1977, pp. 583-603.

Parkin, Andrew. *The Dramatic Imagination of W.B. Yeats*. Dublin: Gill and Macmillan, and New York: Barnes and Noble Books, 1978.

Parkinson, Thomas. *W.B. Yeats: The Later Poetry*. Berkeley: University of California Press, 1964.

------. *W.B. Yeats Self-Critic: A Study of His Early Verse and the Later Poetry*. II Vols. in one. Berkeley: University of California Press, 1971.

Partridge, A.C. *The Language of Modern Poetry: Yeats, Eliot, Auden*. London: Andre Deutsch, 1976.

Raine, Kathleen. "Yeats, The Tarot, and the Golden Dawn." *The Sewanee Review*, Vol. 77, No. 1, Winter 1969, pp. 112-48.

Raines, Charles H. "Yeats's Metaphors of Permanence." *Twentieth-Century Literature*, Vol. 5, April 1959-January 1960 (Kraus rpt. New York, 1965), pp. 12-20.

Rajan, Balachandra. *W.B. Yeats: A Critical Introduction*. 1965; rpt; London: Hutchinson University Library, 1972.

Ransom, John Crowe. "Yeats and His Symbols." *The Kenyon Review*, Vol. I, No. 3, Summer 1939, pp. 309-22.

Rayan, Krishna. "Yeats and the 'Little and Intense' Poem." *Essays in Criticism*, Vol. 25, No. 4, October 1975.

Reeves, James. *The Poets and Their Critics: Arnold to Auden*. London: Hutchinson, 1969.

Reynolds, Lorna. "Collective Intellect: Yeats, Synge and Nietzsche." *Essays and Studies* (1973), pp. 83-98.

Rosenthal, M.L. *The Modern Poets: A Critical Introduction*. New York: OUP, 1965.

------. *Sailing Into the Unknown: Yeats, Pound and Eliot*. New York: OUP, 1978

Rudd, Margaret. *Divided Image: A Study of William Blake and W.B. Yeats*. Routledge and Kegan Paul, 1953.

Savage, D.S. "The Aestheticism of W.B. Yeats." *The Kenyon Review*, Vol. 7, No. 1, Winter 1945, pp. 118-34.

Schmidt, Michael. *A Reader's Guide to Fifty Modern British Poets*. New York: Heinemann, 1979.

Schuler, Robert M. "W.B. Yeats: Artist or Alchemist?" *The Review of English Studies*, 22, No. 85 (February 1971), pp. 37-53.

Snukal, Robert. High Talk: *The Philosophical Poetry of W.B. Yeats*. Cambridge: At the University Press, 1973.

Southam, B.C. "Yeats: Life and the Creator in 'The Long-Legged Fly'." *Twentieth-Century Literature*, Vol. 6, No. 4, Jan. 1961, pp. 175-79.

Stallworthy, Jon. *Between the Lines: Yeats's Poetry in the Making*. 1963; rpt. Oxford: At the Clarendon Press, 1971.

------. *Vision and Revision in Yeats's Last Poems*. Oxford: At the Clarendon Press, 1969.

Stead, C.K. *The New Poetic: Yeats to Eliot*. New York: Harper Torchbooks, 1964.

Stein, Arnold. "Yeats: A Study in Recklessness." *The Sewanee Review*, Vol. 57, No. 4, Autumn 1949, pp. 603-26.

Stewart, J.I.M. *Eight Modern Writers*. (*Oxford History of English Literature*, ed. F.P. Wilson and Bonamy Dobree). 1963; rpt. Oxford: At the Clarendon Press, 1966.

Stock, A.G. *W.B. Yeats: His Poetry and Thought*. 1961; rpt. Cambridge: At the University Press, 1964.

Thompson, Denys. *The Uses of Poetry*. Cambridge: Cambridge University Press, 1978.

Thorton, R.K.R. *The Decadent Dilemma*. London: Edward Arnold, 1983.

Tomlinson, Alan. "W.B. Yeats and Gordon Craig." *Ariel*, Vol. 3, No. 3, July 1972, pp. 48-57.

Tuohy, Frank. *Yeats*. London: Macmillan, 1976.

Unterecker, John. *A Reader's Guide to William Butler Yeats*. 1959; rpt. London: Thames and Hudson, 1969.

Ure, Peter. *Yeats the Playwright: A Commentary on Character and Design in the Major Plays*. 1963; rpt. London: Routledge and Kegan Paul, 1969.

Webster, Brenda S. *Yeats: A Phychoanalytic Study*. London: The Macmillan Press, 1974.

Whitaker, Thomas R. "Yeats's Alembic." *The Sewanee Review*, Vol. 68, No. 4, Autumn 1960, pp. 576-94.

Wilson, Bruce M. "'From Mirror after Mirror': Yeats and Eastern Thought." *Comparative Literature*, Vol. 34, No. 1, Winter 1982, pp. 28-46.

W.B. Yeats: A Critical Anthology. Ed. William H. Pritchard. Middlesex: Penguin Books, 1972.

W.B. Yeats: The Critical Heritage. Ed. A. Norman Jeffares. London: Routledge and Kegan Paul, 1977.

W.B. Yeats: Interviews and Recollections. Ed. E.M. Mikhail, Vol. I and II. London: The Macmillan Press, 1977.

W.B. Yeats: Memoirs (Autobiography-First Draft Journal) Transcribed and edited by Denis Donoghue. London: Macmillan, 1972.

Wilson, F.A.C. *Yeats's Iconography*. 1960; London: Methuen, 1969.

Winters, Yvor. "The Poetry of W.B. Yeats." *Twentieth-Century Literature*, Vol. 6, No. 1,April 1960-January, 1961 (Kraus rpt.), pp. 3-24.

Wright, George T. *The Poet in the Poem: The Personae of Eliot, Yeats and Pound*. New York: Gordian Press, 1974.

Yeats and the Occult. Ed. George Mills Harper. 1975; London: Macmillan, 1976.

Yeats Annual No. 2. Ed. Richard J. Finneran. London: Macmillan, 1983.

Yeats: A Collection of Critical Essays. Ed. John Unterecker. New Jersey: Prentice Hall, 1963.

Yeats: Last Poems. Ed. John Stallworthy. Macmillan, 1968.
Zimmeman, Lee. "Singing Amid Uncertainty: Yeats's Closing Questions." *Yeats's Annual No. 2*, 1983, pp. 35-45.
Zwerdling, Alex. *Yeats and the Heroic Ideal*. London: Peter Owen, 1966.

III Other Works

Abercrombie, Lascelles. *Romanticism*. 1926; London: High Hill Books, 1963.
Abrams, M.H. *The Mirror and the Lamp: Romantic Theory and the Critical Tradition*. London. OUP, 1960.
------. *Natural Supernaturalism: Tradition and Revolution in Romantic Literature*. London. OUP, 1971.
Alur, Janaki Ram. "Arjuna and Hamlet: Two Moral Dilemmas." *Philosophy East and West*, Vol. 18, Nos. 1 and 2, January-April, 1968.
Arnold, Matthew. *Matthew Arnold's Essays in Criticism*. Introduced by G.K. Chesterton. 1906; rpt. London: J.M. Dent, 1969.
Auden, W.H. *The Collected Poetry of W.H. Auden*. New York: Random House, 1945.
Aurobindo. *Essays on the Gita*. Pondicherry, 1972.
Bahadur, K.P. *The Wisdom of Vaisheshika*. New Delhi: Sterling, 1979.
Balint, Michael. *Thrills and Regressions*. London: The Hogarth Press, 1959.
Barfield, Owen. *Poetic Diction: A Study in Meaning*. Introduction by Howard Nemerov. 1928; New York: McGraw-Hill, 1964.
------. *Romanticism Comes of Age*. London: Rudolf Steiner Press, 1944.
------. *Saving the Appearances: A Study in Idolatry*. 1957; New York: Harcourt, Brace, Jovanovich, 1965.
------. *What Coleridge Thought*. London: OUP, 1972.
------. *Worlds Apart: A Dialogue of the 1960's*. London: Faber and Faber, 1963.
Barth, J. Robert. *The Symbolic Imagination: Coleridge and the Romantic Tradition*. Princeton: Princeton University Press, 1977.
Barzun, Jacques. *Classic, Romantic and Modern*. Chicago: The University of Chicago Press, 1961.
Bateson, F.W. *Essays in Critical Dissent*. London: Longman Group, 1972.
Beer, Patricia. *An Introduction to the Metaphysical Poets*. London: Macmillan, 1972.
Benoit, Raymond. *Single Nature's Double Name: The Collectedness of the Conflicting in British and American Romanticism*. Paris: Mouton, 1973.
Bergonzi, Bernard. *The Turn of a Century: Essays on Victorian and Modern English Literature*. London: The Macmillan Press, 1973.
Bewley, Marius. *Masks and Mirrors: Essays in Criticism*. London: Chatto and Windus, 1970.
Blackmur, R.P. *Language as Gesture: Essays in Poetry*. Connecticut: Greenwood Press, 1977.
------. *The Lion and the Honeycomb*. New York: Harcourt, Brace, 1954.

Blake's Poems and Prophecies. Ed. Max Plôwman. 1927; rpt. London: J.M. Dent, 1970.

Bloom et al. *Deconstruction and Criticism*. London: Routledge and Kegan Paul, 1979.

Bloom, Harold. *The Anxiety of Influence: A Theory of Poetry*. New York: OUP, 1973.

Bowra, C.M. *The Creative Experiment*. London: Macmillan, 1967.

------. *The Romantic Imagination*. 1950; Oxford: OUP, 1978.

Bradbury, Malcolm. "An Age of Parody: Style in the Modern Arts." *Encounter*, Vol. 55, No. 1, July 1980 pp. 36-53.

------. "Struggling Westward: America and the Coming of Modernism." *Encounter* (I), Vol. 60, No. 1, January 1983, pp. 55-60.

------. "Struggling Westward: America and the Coming of Modernism." *Encounter* (II), Vol. 60, No. 2, February 1983, pp. 57-65.

Bridgwater, Patrick. *Nietzsche in Anglosaxony: A Study of Nietzsche's Impact on English and American Literature*. Leicester: Leicester University Press, 1972.

Brome, Vincent. *Jung*. 1978; London: Granada Publishing, 1980.

------. *A Shaping Joy: Studies in the Writer's Craft*. London: Methuen, 1971.

Brooks, Cleanth. *The Well-Wrought Urn*. London: Dennis Dobson, 1968.

Brown, Marshall. "The Pre-Romantic Discovery of Consciousness." *Studies in Romanticism*, Vol. 17, No. 4, Fall 1978, pp. 387-412.

Bruns, Gerald L. *Modern Poetry and the Idea of Language: A Critical and Historical Study*. New Haven: Yale University Press, 1974.

Buckley, Vincent. *Poetry and the Sacred*. London: Chatto and Windus, 1968.

Bullough, Geoffrey. *Mirror of Minds: Changing Psychological Beliefs in English Poetry*. London: The Athlone Press, 1962.

Burnshaw, Stanley. *The Seamless Web: Language--Thinking--Culture--Knowledge--Art--Experience*. London: The Penguin Press, 1970.

Bush, Douglas. *English Poetry: The Main Currents from Chaucer to the Present*. 2nd edition, 1952; rpt. London: Methuen, 1968.

Capra, Fritjof. *The Turning Point: Sceince, Society and the Rising Culture*. Toronto: Bantam Books, 1983.

Cassirer, Ernest. *An Essay on Man: An Introduction to a Philosophy of Human Culture*. New Haven and London: Yale University Press, 1944.

Coleridge, S.T. *Biographia Literaria*. Ed. George Watson. 1975; rpt. London: J.M. Dent, 1977.

Collins, A.S. *English Literature of the Twentieth-Century*. 1951; London: University Tutorial Press, 1965.

Danto, Arthur C. *Sartre*. 1975; rpt. Glasgow: Fontana/Collins, 1981.

Deutsch, Babette. *Poetry in Our Time*. 1951; rpt. New York: Columbia University Press, 1958.

Dictionary of the History of Ideas. Ed. Philip P. Wiener. New York: Scribner's, 1973.

Donne, John. *The Poems of John Donne*. Ed. Sir H.J.C. Grierson. rpt. London: OUP, 1945.

Donoghue, Denis. *The Sovereign Ghost: Studies in Imagination*. London: Faber and Faber, 1978.

Drew, Elizabeth. (In Collaboration with John L. Sweeney). *Directions in Modern Poetry*. 1940; rpt. New York: Gordian Press, 1967.

Eliot, T.S. *Collected Plays*. London: Faber and Faber, 1962.

------. *On Poetry and Poets*. London: Faber and Faber, 1957.

------. *The Sacred Wood: Essays on Poetry and Criticism*. 1920; rpt. London: Methuen, 1969.

------. *Selected Essays*. 1932; London: Faber and Faber, 1972.

------. *Selected Prose*. Ed. John Hayward. 1953; rpt. Middlesex: Penguin Books in association with Faber and Faber, 1955.

Encyclopedia of Poetry and Poetics. Ed. Alex Preminger. 1965; rpt. Princeton: Princeton University Press, 1966.

The Essential Matthew Arnold. Ed. Lionel Trilling. London: Chatto and Windus, 1949.

Evans, B. Ifor. *English Literature Between the Wars*. 2nd Edition, 1948; London: Methuen, 1949.

The Faber Book of Modern Verse. Ed. Michael Roberts. 3rd edition, rev. and with a new supplement of poems chosen by Donald Hall. 1936; rpt. London: Faber and Faber, 1968.

Fordham, Frieda. *An Introduction to Jung's Psychology*. 1953; rpt. Middlesex: Penguin Books, 1982.

Frank, Joseph. *The Widening Gyre: Crisis and Mastery in Modern Literature*. Bloomington: Indiana University Press, 1963.

------. *The Stubborn Structure: Essays on Criticism and Society*. London: Methuen, 1970.

Frye, Northrop. *A Study of English Romanticism*. Sussex: The Harvester Press, 1983.

Gillie, Christopher. *Movements in English Literature: 1900-1940*. 1975; rpt. Cambridge: Cambridge University Press, 1978.

Gordon, Lyndall. *Eliot's Early Years*. Oxford: OUP, 1977.

Grierson, Herbert J.C. and Smith, J.C. *A Critical History of English Poetry*. 1944; rpt. London: Chatto and Windus, 1970.

Gross, Harvey. *The Contrived Corridor: History and Fatality in Modern Literature*. Michigan: University of Michigan Press, 1971.

Gunn, Giles B. *Literature and Religion*. London: S.C.M. Press, 1971.

Gunter, Pete A. "Nietzschean Laughter." *The Sewanee Review*, Vol. 76, No. 3, Summer 1968, pp. 493-506.

Heller, Erich. *The Disinherited Mind: Essays in Modern German Literature and Thought*. London: Bowes and Bowes, 1971.

Henn, T.R. *The Harvest of Tragedy*. London: Methuen, 1956.

Hobsbaum, Philip. *Tradition and Experiment in English Poetry*. London: The

Macmillan Press, 1979.
Holbrook, David. *Liareggub Revisited: Dylan Thomas and the State of Modern Poetry*. 1962; Bath: Cedric Chivers, 1974.
Hough, Graham. *Image and Experience: Studies in a Literary Revolution*. London: Gerald Duckworth, 1960.
Hughson, Lois. *Thresholds of Reality: George Santayana and Modernist Poetics*. National University Publications, Kennikot Press, 1977.
I.A. Richards: Essays in His Honour. Ed. Reuben Brower, Helen Vendler and John Hollander. New York: OUP, 1973.
Interpretations: The Poetry of Meaning. Ed. Stanley Romaine Hopper and David L. Miller. New York: Harcourt, Brace and World, 1967.
James, D.G. *The Romantic Comedy: An Essay on English Romanticism*. London: OUP, 1963.
Joyce, James. *A Portrait of the Artist as a Young Man*. 1916; rpt. Middlesex: Penguin Books, 1976.
Jung, Carl Gustav. *Psychology and Religion*. New Haven: Yale University Press, 1938.
------. *The Undiscovered Self*. Trans. R.F.C. Hull. London: Routledge and Kegan Paul, 1958.
Kakonis, Thomas E., et al. *The Literary Artist as Social Critic*. California Glencoe Press, 1969.
Kramer, Lawrence "The Return of the Gods: Keats to Rilke." *Studies in Romanticism*, Vol. 17, No. 4, Fall 1978, pp. 483-85.
Krieger, Murray. *The Classic Vision: The Retreat from Extremity*. 1971; Baltimore and London: The Johns Hopkins University Press, 1973.
------. *The New Apologists for Poetry*. Bloomington: Indiana University Press, 1963.
------. "Poetics Reconstructed: The Presence Versus the Absence of the Word." *NLH*, Vol. 7, No. 2, Winter 1976, pp. 347-75.
------. *Theory of Criticism: A Tradition and Its System*. 1976; rpt. Baltimore: The Johns Hopkins University Press, 1981.
------. *The Tragic Vision: Variations on a Theme in Literary Interpretation*. 1960; Chicago: The University of Chicago Press, 1966.
Krutch, Joseph Wood. *Experience and Art: Some Aspects of the Aesthetics of Literature*. New York: Collier Books, 1962.
Langbaum, Robert. *The Modern Spirit: Essays on the Continuity of Nineteenth and Twentieth Century Literature*. 1959; New York: OUP, 1970.
Lewis, C. Day. *The Poetic Image*. The Clark Lectures given at Cambridge in 1946. London: Jonathan Capoa, 1947.
Literature and Religion. Ed. Giles B. Gunn. London. S.C.M. Press, 1971.
Literature and Western Civilisation: The Modern World II Realities. Gen. Ed. David Daiches and Anthony Thorlby. London: Aldus Books, 1972.
Lobb, Edward. *T.S. Eliot and the Romantic Critical Tradition*. London: Routledge and Kegan Paul, 1981.

Lucas, F.L. *Style*. 7th Ed. 1955; London: Cassell, 1964.

MacLeish. *Poetry and Experience*. London: The Bodley Head, 1961.

Man and His Symbols. Ed. Carl G. Jung. 1964, rpt. London: Picador, 1983.

Maritain, Jacques and Raissa. *The Situation of Poetry: Four Essays on the Relations between Poetry, Mysticism, Magic and Knowledge*. New York: Philosophical Library, 1955.

Marsh, Robert. *Four Dialectical Theories of Poetry: An Aspect of English Neoclassical Criticism*. Chicago: The University of Chicago Press, 1965.

Martin, Wallace. "The Hermeneutic Circle and the Art of Interpretation." *Comparative Literature*, Vol. 24, No. 2, Spring 1972, pp. 97-117.

Mason, Michael. *The Centre of Hilarity: A Play Upon Ideas about Laughter and the Absurd*. London: Sheed and Ward, 1959.

Matthiessen, F.O. *The Achievements of T.S. Eliot: An Essay on the Nature of Poetry*. New York: A Galaxy Book, 1959.

Mazzaro, Jerome. *Transformations in the Renaissance English Lyric*. Ithaca: Cornell University Press, 1970.

Meakin, David. *Man and Work: Literature and Culture in Industrial Society*. London: Methuen, 1976.

Miles, Josephine. *Poetry and Change: Donne, Milton, Wordsworth, and the Equilibrium of the Present*. California: University of California Press, 1974.

Modern Continental Literary Criticism. Ed. O.B. Hardison, Jr. New York: The University of North Carolina, Appleton-Century-Crofts, Educational Division. Meridity Corporation, 1962.

The Modern Tradition: Backgrounds of Modern Literature. Ed. Richard Ellmann and Charles Feidelson. New York: OUP, 1965.

Morrison, Blake. *The Movement: English Poetry and Fiction of the 1950s*. Oxford: OUP, 1980.

Muir, Edwin. *The Estate of Poetry*. London: The Hogarth Press, 1962.

Mumford, Lewis. *Interpretations and Forecasts: 1922-1972: Studies in Literature, History, Biography, Technics and Contemporary Society*. London: Secker and Warburg, 1973.

The New Golden Treasury of English Verse. Chosen by Edward Leeson. London: Pan Books, in association with Macmillan London, 1983.

O'Brien, Connor Cruise. *The Suspecting Glance*. London: Faber and Faber, 1972.

The Oxford Anthology of English Literature, Vol. II Ed. Frank Kermode and John Hollander. London: OUP, 1973.

Paz, Octavio. *Children of the Mire: Modern Poetry from Romanticism to the Avant-Garde*. Trans. Rachel Phillips. 1974; rpt. Massachusetts: Harvard University Press, 1975.

Pinto, Vivian De Sola. *Crisis in English Poetry: 1880-1940*. 3rd ed. 1951; London: Hutchinson University Library, 1958.

The Poems of Gerard Manley Hopkins. (4th ed. based on the 1st ed. of 1918). Ed.

W.H. Gardner and N.H. Mackenzie. Oxford: OUP, 1970.

Press, John. *The Chequer'd Shade: Reflections on Obscurity in Poetry*. London: OUP, 1963.

------. *The Fire and the Fountain: An Essay on Poetry*. London: OUP, 1955.

------. *The Lengthening Shadows*. London: OUP, 1971.

------. *A Map of Modern English Verse*. London: OUP, 1969.

Pritchard, Williams H. *Lives of the Modern Poets*. London: Faber and Faber, 1980.

Psychoanalysis, Creativity, and Literature: A French-American Inquiry. Ed. Alan Roland. New York: Columbia Univesity Press, 1978.

Rand, Ayn. *The Romantic Manifesto: A Philosophy of Literature*. 2nd Revised ed. 1971; New York: A Signet Book, 1975.

Read, Herbert. *The Cult of Sincerity*. London: Faber and Faber, 1968.

------. *The Forms of Things Unknown*. London: Faber and Faber, 1960.

------. *The Tenth Muse: Essays in Criticism*. London: Routledge and Kegan Paul, 1957.

------. *The True Voice of Feeling: Studies in English Romantic Poetry*. London: Faber and Faber, 1968.

Reichert, John. "Do Poets ever Mean What They Say?." *NLH*, Vol. XIII, No. 1, Autumn, 1981.

Reid, B.L. *Tragic Occasions: Essay on Several Forms*. New York: National University Publications; Kennikat Press, 1971.

Richards, I.A. *Coleridge on Imagination*. 1934; rpt. London. Routledge and Kegan Paul, 1968.

------. *Poetries and Sciences. A Reissue of Science and Poetry*. (1926, 1935), London: Routledge and Kegan Paul, 1970.

------. *Principles of Literary Criticism*. rpt. London: Routledge and Kegan Paul, 1976.

Robson, W.W. *Modern English Literature*. London: OUP, 1970.

Sankaracaraya's *Self-Knowledge* (Atma Bodha), Trans. Swami Nikhilananda. Madras: Sri Ramakrishna Math, 1978.

A Sanskrit-English Dictionary. Etymologically and Philologically arranged with special reference to cognate Indo-European Languages by Sir Monier-Monier-Williams. New ed. with collaboration of Professor E. Leuman and Professor C. Cappeller et al. 1899: New Delhi, Motilal Banarsidass, 1970.

Santayana, George. *The Sense of Beauty: Being the Outline of Aesthetic Theory*. New York: Collier Books, 1961.

Schenk, H.G. *The Mind of the European Romantics: An Essay in Cultural History*. Preface by Isaiah Berlin. 1966; Oxford: OUP, 1979.

Scott, Wilbur. *Five Approaches of Literary Criticism: An Arrangement of Contemporary Critical Essays*. 1962; rpt. New York: Collier Books, 1977.

Selected Prose of T.S. Eliot. Ed. Frank Kermode. London: Faber and Faber, 1975.

A Selection from Scrutiny. Comp. F.R. Leavis. 2 Vols. Cambridge: At the University Press, 1968.

Selections From Wordsworth: Poetry and Prose. Ed. Sir Ifor Evans. 11th ed. 1935; London: Methuen, 1966.

Shakespeare, William. *Shakespeare: Complete Works*. Ed. W.J. Craig. 1905; rpt. Oxford: OUP, 1980.

Shapiro, Karl. *The Poetry Wreck: Selected Essays: 1950-1970*. New York: Random House, 1975.

Shawcross, J. Ed. *Biographia Literaria* by S.T. Coleridge (ed. with his aesthetical essays), Vol. I, Ist ed. 1907; rpt. London: OUP, 1967.

Sisson, C.H. *English Poetry 1900-1950: An Assessment*. London: Rupert Hart-Davis, 1971.

Skelton, Robin. *Poetic Truth*. London: Heinemann, New York: Barnes and Noble, Agincourt: The Book Society of Canada, 1978.

Spender, Stephen. *The Making of a Poem*. London: Hamish Hamilton, 1955.

Stanford, W.B. *Enemies of Poetry*. London: Routledge and Kegan Paul, 1980.

Stein, Walter. *Criticism as Dialogue*. Cambridge: At the University Press, 1969.

Stern, J.P. *Nietzsche*. 1978; Glasgow: Fontana/Collins, 1981.

Stevens, Wallace. *The Collected Poems of Wallace Stevens*. 1955; rpt. London: Faber and Faber, 1966.

Storr, Anthony. *Jung*. 1973; rpt. Glasgow: Fontana, 1982.

Swiatecka, M. Jadwiga. *The Idea of the Symbol: Some Nineteenth Century Comparisons with Coleridge*. Cambridge: Cambridge Univ. Press, 1980.

Tate, Allen. *The Man of Letters in the Modern World: Selected Essays: 1928-55*. 1955; rpt. Cleveland: The World Publishing, 1964.

Topics in Criticism: An Ordered Set of Positions in Literary Theory. Arranged by Christopher Butler and Alastair Fowler. 1971; rpt. Longman, 1978.

Toynbee, Arnold. *The World and the West*. London: OUP, 1952.

Trilling, Lionel. *Sincerity and Authenticity*. 1971; rpt. Cambridge: Harvard University Press, 1973.

Twentieth Century Literature in Restrospect. Harvard English Studies-2. Ed. Reuben A. Brower. Cambridge: Harvard Univ. Press, 1971.

Warner, Francis. *Studies in the Arts*. Oxford: Basil Blackwell, 1968.

------. *Democracy and Poetry*. The 1974 Jefferson Lecture in the Humanities. Harvard: Harvard Univ. Press, 1975.

Warren, Robert Penn. *Selected Essays*. New York, 1958.

Wellek, Rene. *The Attack on Literature and Other Essays*. Sussex: The Harvester Press, 1982.

Whitehead, Alfred North. *Science and the Modern World: Lowell Lectures, 1925*. New York: Mentor Books; 1956.

Wilson, Colin. *The Outsider*. London: Pan Books, 1963.

------. *Poetry and Mysticism*. Hutchinson, London, 1970.

Wolf, Ernest S. "Psychoanalytic Psychology of the Self and Literature." *NLH*, Vol. XII, No. 1, Autumn 1980, pp. 41-60.

Wollheim, Richard. *Freud*. 1971; rpt. Glasgow: Fontana, 1982.

Index